BULLETPROOF

BY MACI BOOKOUT

A POST HILL PRESS BOOK
ISBN (trade paperback): 978-1-68261-283-5
ISBN (hardcover): 978-1-61868-864-4
ISBN (eBook): 978-1-61868-865-1

BULLETPROOF

Cover Photo by Carrie Workman, Carrie Workman Photography

Post Hill Press
posthillpress.com

Published in the United States of America

DEDICATION

I dedicate this book to the ones
who helped create my story.
Mom, for being my foundation that never shook;
Daddy, for loving me even when I didn't;
Matt, for always being there;
And Bentley. You brought me to life,
and made this life worth living.

CONTENTS

CONTENTS

INTRODUCTION

I always wanted to write a book, but I never imagined it would happen quite like this. Writing has always been my own private passion, a way of expressing feelings and thoughts I didn't know how to share with others, or simply wanted to keep to myself. Back when I was a teenager, before my life started tumbling toward where it is today, I used to love spending my nights alone in my room, listening to music and writing. I've always been a bit reserved, never one to express all of my thoughts out loud. Through written words, whether it's the lyrics of a favorite song or my own poetry, I can let my feelings take shape. But still, for years, I kept it all mostly to myself. Until now.

To some of you, it might sound strange for me to speak of myself as if I'm a private person. Over the seven years leading up to the publication of this book, I've lived large parts of my life on camera as a subject of MTV's documentary series *16 & Pregnant* and *Teen Mom*. If you're one of the millions of viewers who got to know me as "Maci from MTV," you've seen a lot of me through camera lenses (and perhaps in the pages of magazines or gossip websites). But no matter how "real" a documentary tries to be, there are always differences between the way things look on camera and the way they actually are. I know that's true in my case. When I saw myself on screen for the first time, I was surprised by how calm I appeared on the surface in situations that I remembered as total chaos. Over the years it became clear to me that I wasn't able to show a complete view of my story through my appearances on camera. I wondered if, without meaning to, I had misled people into thinking teen motherhood and all the struggles that came with it were easier for me than they actually were.

That's why I wanted to write this book. Because a journey like mine looks much different from behind the wheel, and for me, the whole truth flows much more easily onto a page. This is the best way I know to shed light on the real feelings, conflicts, challenges, and victories I wasn't able to communicate in front of the cameras, or even, sometimes, in front of my closest friends and family. This is my way of showing what was really happening beneath the surface of "Maci from MTV."

This is the story of a regular teenage girl who found herself with a life she never expected -- two lives, to be exact. From the moment I found out I was pregnant at sixteen years old to the birth of my son Bentley, from my troubled engagement to Bentley's father to the downfall of that first love, from struggling with overwhelming loneliness to reclaiming my independence, the journey was long, hard, and packed full of lessons.

It wasn't until I began writing this book that I realized just how much I had learned and how much I had to share. My only hope is to let you see what things were really like for me during those crazy years. Not only as a teen mom, and not only as an MTV celebrity, but as a young woman struggling to find her own strength, maintain her independence, and establish a positive, happy life, even in the midst of overwhelming challenges and intimidating odds.

If you've been in shoes like mine, or if you're in a place where you could be, I hope you can share in the lessons I learned without having to learn them yourself the hard way. I hope my story helps you not to feel as alone as I often felt. And if you've never been in my shoes, even if you never will be, I hope it helps you understand what it's really like to walk this path, for me and for so many others.

Finally, I want to thank you. To those of you who have been following my journey all these years, thank you. Thank you for taking an interest in my life, my journey, and my story. Thank you for wanting to understand. Thank you for giving me the chance to show you, as best I can, what it's really like to be Maci.

CHAPTER 1:

LIFE BEFORE LIFE

At sixteen years old, I was not looking for a relationship. Finding a boyfriend was so far down on my list of things to do, it didn't even have its own number. All around me, my friends and classmates were getting their feet wet in their first real relationships. Some were casual and some were serious, but they all seemed to involve a lot of drama. Fighting, cheating, codependency, jealousy, obsession — pretty much the full spectrum of unpleasant emotions, and as far as I could tell, most of them weren't even in love! To me it seemed like the majority of people in high school were getting boyfriends or girlfriends because it was just the cool thing to do. And I just didn't think it was a good look for me.

Back then, I liked being alone. Not all the time, or anything. My days were full of social activities from softball to cheerleading and hanging out with the same big group of friends I'd had since middle school. But at night, I was happy by myself at the computer, looking up new music, reading lyrics, and writing poetry. I could literally do that for hours. There was no blank space in my life begging for a relationship, and I was happy not to risk looking like a dumbass with the wrong boyfriend. I was doing just fine on my own.

Not only that, but I wanted to do just fine on my own. I always preferred to take care of my own business. I can probably thank my mom for that. When I was growing up, there were three or four occasions where she went out of her way to show me how to do some kind of "guy thing," like fixing a leaky pipe or changing a flat tire. I remember each time it happened because of what she said: "I'm teaching you how to do this so you'll never need a man to do it for you." It doesn't get more practical than that. Of course, if a man wants to help, that's great. But you can't be sure he'll be around for every flat tire. Or even that he'll know what to do any more than you do.

The lesson stuck with me. Maybe even to a fault. For as long as I can remember, I've been quick to say, "I can do this. I don't need you to do it for me."

It was working out pretty well for me at sixteen. Life was good. I lived in Chattanooga, where I was born and raised. My parents were high school sweethearts who had their first kid, my older brother Matt, when they were just teenagers. I was born a few years later. My parents were younger than a lot of my friends' parents, and they seemed even younger together. I remember watching them bicker and squabble in the kitchen, acting like they were still two feisty teenagers in love. Hilarious and so cute.

We were a close family. The four of us were constantly together, going camping or taking trips to the beach, and every night we sat down at the dinner table together. I'm always thankful for those family dinners, where we had an hour to sit and talk to each other about our days and what we had going on in our lives. It helped to keep us close and bonded as the years went by. We're not the types to be up in each other's business all the time. Growing up, as long as I was respectful and followed the rules, my parents trusted me to be myself and do my own thing.

Chattanooga was a great place to grow up. It's a beautiful place, all mountains and trees and slow-paced Southern charm. People are nice and laid-back, and there's always something to do outside. As a kid I was always outdoors, usually either riding dirt bikes or playing softball. I was obsessed with softball. I started playing softball when I was just four years old, and it was love at first practice. By the time I was ten, it was a year-round occupation. Since I didn't have real plans to play in college or beyond, it was a passion with an expiration date. High school graduation would be the end of my softball career, so I was extra passionate about it, because I didn't want to waste a minute of the time I had to play the game while I was young.

As for dirt bikes, there wasn't much of a future for me in that passion, either. But I had another interest I hoped to turn into a career: cooking. When I was little, I used to watch the Food Network instead of watching cartoons. I begged my parents to let me use the stove before I could even reach it properly, so I could make myself fried okra for an afternoon snack. Every time I saw one of the chefs on TV making something that looked really good, I'd make my mom take me to the store so I could get all of the ingredients and try it out. Pasta dishes were easy for me to understand, and as I got older, I got into desserts and learning to make cookies and cakes from scratch. I was lucky enough to have at my high school a home economics class, which I'm not even sure exists anymore. I was always on the roster, and by the time I was a junior I was making plans to try for the culinary program at the Art Institute of Atlanta. I did a big school project that involved working in a restaurant, and I went down to the school to take a cooking course. I had everything all lined up.

All in all, I felt like I had things under control as a teenager. Who needed a boyfriend?

But we all know how it goes. Famous last words.

Blame it on dirt bikes. That's how I met Ryan, in a roundabout way. There's a whole social network surrounding motocross. The same people gather over the years at local tracks, and the same crowds travel from state to state for different events. Faces become

familiar, even friendly. One day I learned there was someone who
wanted to get friendly and familiar with me. His name was Ryan,
my friend Abbey told me over the phone. He was best friends with
her boyfriend. All of them spent time at the local motocross track.
Ryan had seen me there several times, and he'd been asking around
about me.

"This guy likes you," Abbey said. "He thinks you're really pretty."

"Oh, really?" I went straight to MySpace, which was how you
stalked people in those days. I was pleasantly surprised. Ryan was
older, and he was seriously good looking.

"We should all hang out sometime soon," Abbey suggested.

"Sure," I said. Yeah, yeah. I wasn't looking for a boyfriend. But
the sight of Ryan didn't exactly make me want to run for the hills,
either. You can't blame a girl.

Curiosity (or human weakness) aside, I was still iffy on the
idea of dating. Honestly, I was just afraid it would turn out to be a
pain in the ass. But as it turned out, Ryan was hard to resist. From
the first moment we properly met in June, he gave me all of his
attention. And I was careful not to lead him on. I made it clear
that I wasn't sure if I wanted to get involved with anyone. But he
took it in stride. We spent more and more time together, usually in
groups of friends, and his eyes were always on me. Even though
I wasn't giving him the kind of relationship he wanted, his focus
never wavered. There was no game, no drama. He just liked me,
and so he kept trying. And trying. And trying.

I had to admit, it was cute.

Ryan was a nice guy with a charming attitude and a little bit
of an edge. He came from a good family and he knew how to
treat people well. And he was older, so he had an atmosphere of
knowing who he was and what he wanted that I found appealing.
There was no question I was attracted to him, and his effort was

hard to ignore. Little by little, my reservations about high school romance started to thaw. A few months in, I realized it was time to admit that I had feelings for him, too. By the time October rolled around, we were officially a couple.

Having a boyfriend was nothing like what I'd feared. We had the most easygoing relationship in the world, although we did spend much less time together than a lot of couples our age. Ryan was already out of school and had a job as a diesel mechanic. He worked the night shift during the week, so our only time to meet was in the afternoon when I was out of school. We'd meet somewhere nearby and grab a bite to eat at Sonic before he started his shift. And on the weekends we'd go ride four-wheelers, get dinner, go to the movies, or hang out with friends.

We were in the honeymoon phase, and it was good. We were that annoying, over-infatuated couple our friends rolled their eyes at. It was a total rush. We had no conflicts, no trust issues, no mind games, no arguments. We also weren't talking about the future. But I didn't see anything wrong with living in the moment. We were in love. We were happy. And our chemistry was off the charts.

I have never been a promiscuous type, but I wasn't a prude, either. I didn't fool around with anyone, but I talked about sex with my girlfriends like any normal teenager. I didn't plan to wait for marriage, but I had my own standards in mind. I just wanted sex to be on my terms. I didn't want to do it until I wanted it so bad I couldn't stand to say no. I didn't want to wake up the next day and regret having sex. I wanted a situation where the idea was so attractive to me that I'd be afraid to wake up and regret not having had sex. That was my standard. I wanted it when I wanted it, and not a second sooner.

I was into Ryan. Plain and simple. It was the first time I'd
ever felt such an immediate, undeniable attraction to someone. It's
funny how that happens. There are so many nice, attractive people
you meet in your life and never feel particularly drawn to. But then
once in awhile, someone comes along and it's almost like a shot of
love potion. There's no rhyme or reason to having such a strong
feeling about someone you don't even know yet. I was too young
to figure out how much was love and how much was lust. Then
again, I don't know if anyone can really tell the difference right
off the bat. Whatever the science behind it may be, sparks flew
between Ryan and me and I loved it.

I never felt pressured into sex. If anything, it was the other way
around. Things were passionate between us, but when we started
to get ourselves into hotter and heavier situations, we'd ease up by
shifting into conversation. "I'm okay with it, you know," I'd say.
"If it happens, it happens." But he didn't want me to do anything
that I'd regret. I'm sure there was an element of chivalry involved.
At the same time, I wondered if he was a little afraid I'd lose some
of my good girl appeal if I slept with him. Purity can be a turn-on,
you know, just like modesty.

But after three or four months of dating, I didn't give a damn
about either one of those. My hormones were racing and I couldn't
take it anymore. My only condition for losing my virginity was that
I wanted to be sure about it. Well, now I was sure. Completely
sure. And once it was done, I had exactly zero regrets. We were
young and in love, and we had a lot of fun.

I never drank a sip of alcohol in high school. I never smoked
cigarettes. I never did drugs. But I might have gotten a little high
on life when I was with my boyfriend. We took full advantage
of our time together at every chance we got. And we felt more
attracted to each other than ever. We couldn't get enough of each

other. The time we spent together seemed more intense. Since we couldn't enjoy ourselves fully with our friends around, I started seeing him more alone, which always feels more meaningful, in a way. Our relationship felt deeper because of it, or at least I thought so. At any rate, I had no complaints. I felt like I had it all.

CHAPTER 2:

10 LESSONS I LEARNED FROM MY MOM

1. Live up to your own standards, even when people underestimate you.

Since my dad was usually with my brother at motocross or wrestling events, my mom took care of me and softball. This was one of many lessons she taught me during those drives to and from tryouts, practice, games. My biggest challenge in softball was that I was very petite and always playing with bigger, stronger girls. There were times when even though I was the more skilled player, coaches would pass me up for someone with an intimidation factor. On one hand I was always being told that I was really good, and on the other hand that I was too small to play the game. It was a constant struggle to maintain my confidence, but my mom would hammer it in: "Don't listen to them. You know how good you are, you just have to stay focused and keep showing them what you can do." Instead of being discouraged, I gave it my all and left softball feeling accomplished.

2. Try your best not to be the reason someone is upset.

It may be a cliché, but my mom taught me to treat others the way I want to be treated. I've always tried as hard as I can to be kind and respectful, and I do believe it's why I've so rarely had to deal with anyone bullying me or being mean. What makes it easier to be kind is that she taught me to think about the reasons people might have for their views and behavior. You never know what someone else is going through when they get home. Even if they're being mean to you, you don't have to stoop down to what they're doing. Nobody wants to be mean and unhappy. Everyone has their own struggles, and even if you don't know what the problem is, you should always try your best to make sure that it isn't you.

3. If you want things to turn out well, you better work for it.

My mom had my brother when she was seventeen, but didn't let it stop her from getting her GED. She had me at twenty, and worked full time. By the time she was twenty-four, she graduated from college with a Bachelor's Degree, on the Dean's List. (There's a picture of me, my mom, my dad and my brother at her graduation, her with her crazy perm!) She was able to build a career while raising a family, and thirty years later, she's set to retire from the same job she started with. From a teen mom perspective, that's as inspiring as it gets. Anytime I wanted to slack off in school or felt like I just couldn't handle all my obligations, I'd think "Mom got it done, and she did it fast, and she did it without a TV show. And if she did it, I can do it."

4. Learn how to be independent, and never forget.

It's not just about men, but in all areas of life. It doesn't matter how much people are willing to help you or how much you appreciate it. You should always work to be capable of handling problems yourself before turning to others for help. Not only does it make you a more confident and well-rounded person, but it gives you the strength to make choices even when they might mean losing a measure of comfort or assistance you've become dependent on. Besides, if you're surrounded by a wonderful group of friends, family, and a great partner who would all race to your side should you need them, wouldn't you want to know that you're just as capable of helping if they need you someday?

5. Respect yourself and know your worth.

This comes from both my mom and my dad, and what I learned from their relationship. They had their struggles and arguments, but there was always a level of respect between the two of them. One was never scornful or dismissive of the other's feelings or views. When my mom felt she wasn't getting an equal level of respect, she demanded it, and my dad paid it. It helped me understand that if you don't demand that level of respect, it can easily slide away. Watching them interact with each other, I saw that she was demanding it and he was man enough to give it to her. So at the same time, I learned from my dad that that's what I needed to look for in a partner. It's thanks to them that I know my standards for how I'll accept being treated and spoken to.

6. You always need a back-up plan.

She'll know what that means.

7. Don't say it's impossible until Mom has tried it.

I don't know how many times it was seven in the morning before a softball game and I couldn't find my socks. I'd comb every inch of my room and turn it upside down before I'd go downstairs swearing I'd looked everywhere in the world. She'd say, "Really?" And then she'd sigh, walk upstairs, and find my socks in two seconds. It always blew my mind. It wasn't just socks. If I feel like I've looked everywhere for a solution to a problem and I still can't figure it out, I know my mom will suggest something I haven't considered and make it seem like the most obvious thing in the world. Also, years later, I was getting my son ready for baseball practice and he swore his socks were nowhere to be found. I asked, "Really?" And I sighed, walked in, and found them in two seconds.

8. You can be a parent and a friend.

People always say you should be a parent and not a friend, but my mom always seemed to have the perfect balance of both. I always thought of her and respected her as my mom. But I could also talk to her about things that some teenagers would only talk to their friends about. I always felt like even if she might not want to hear what I had to say or she wasn't thrilled to have some awkward conversation with me, I knew I could be open without her judging me or being angry. She always knew when to listen as a mom and when to listen as a friend. Because of that, I know to constantly make sure Bentley knows that he can come to me and talk to me about anything at all without feeling like what he thinks, feels, or says is going to change how I feel about him. My mom always kept a line of communication open in a very nonjudgmental way, and she's my best friend to this day. Frankly, when I want to spend the day drinking beer and talking and having a good time, I go hang out with my parents.

9. Your lipstick only looks as good as the words coming out of your mouth.

It's another cliché to say that inner beauty is more important than outer beauty, but I'm glad my mom never focused on my appearance. She let me dress the way I wanted to. If I wanted to wear makeup she let me, and if I didn't want to wear makeup, she had nothing to say about it. She was never the type of mom to say,

"Why are you wearing that? It's ugly." If I wanted to put on my brother's Teenage Mutant Ninja Turtles tee shirt with some pink shorts and two different shoes, that was fine with her. She was way more concerned with the kind of person I turned out to be on the inside, and so that's what I learned to care about, too. I think I look better with makeup, but I don't think twice about going without it. But I will freak out if I think I've acted in a way that makes me look like a dumbass.

10. When you find a good partner, let him be a good partner.

For all she taught me about being independent, she also taught me to let people in. And that includes your romantic partner. You should never feel like you can't live without a man, but when you do find a good one, you have to let him be good. You don't have to keep proving yourself all the time or reminding him that you don't need him. Let him take care of you and let yourself enjoy it. That's what he needs if he loves you, and that's what you should appreciate in a partnership. Be independent, but don't be too stubborn about it for your own good.

CHAPTER 3:

THE DAY MY LIFE BEGAN

It was a Saturday morning just like any other Saturday morning... until it wasn't.

When I got up that day, I had no reason to think anything crazy was about to happen. I hadn't had any weird dreams. I didn't feel a sixth sense tingling. I was just minding my own business, rolling out of bed and auto-walking into the shower to start my morning. I bet I wouldn't even have remembered that day if I hadn't almost puked.

The wave of nausea hit me out of nowhere as I stepped under the spray, and it was major. My stomach rolled so hard I had to get out and sit next to the toilet, convinced I was about to throw up. I stayed there for a few minutes, not even moving, frozen in that horrible waiting-to-puke zone. But then, to my relief, the feeling passed and I felt fine.

I shrugged it off and got back to my business, still barely even awake. I figured I'd just gotten out of bed too fast, that maybe I'd moved around too much before my body had a chance to adjust. But when I stepped back into the shower, I had another problem: the water was killing my boobs. I couldn't blame the shower; the water pressure was the same as usual. I didn't know what to blame. I didn't have any bruises. I wasn't on my period. There was no reason why I shouldn't be able to handle a bit of water on my chest. But I couldn't! I spent half the shower with my back turned to the spray. That's how tender my boobs were all of a sudden.

I tried to shrug that off, too. But as I woke up, my brain started connecting the dots for me without even asking my permission. By the time I turned off the water, I knew.

I was pregnant.

I just knew it.

Of course, there's knowing and there's knowing. This was the kind that's easier to keep to yourself. Even though I had a feeling in my gut, I tried to push it all the way out of my head. I'm all about trusting your intuition and everything, but this one seemed kind of...well, insane. There was just no way, I thought. I wasn't that type of girl. That sort of thing would never happen to me.

The bottom line was, I didn't say anything to anyone about my shower epiphany. Not one word. To be honest, I barely even said anything to myself about it! Call it denial or call it procrastination, but I spent that weekend deliberately ignoring the elephant in the room. Unfortunately, I couldn't keep that up for long.

When Monday rolled around, it felt like that elephant was sitting right on top of me. The anxiety of it was stifling. It was all I could think about: I'm pregnant. I'm pregnant. I'm pregnant. It took a lot of will power to make it through the motions of a normal day, making my way through the hallways amid all the usual sights and sounds of lockers shutting, friends hollering and bells ringing us in and out of class. Because the entire time, I knew something was off. And as crazy as it seemed, as much as it pained me to think about it, I knew what that something was. And I knew my shut-your-eyes, plug-your-ears strategy couldn't go on forever. It was time to face what my instincts were telling me and get myself a damn pregnancy test.

At the time, for some reason, I thought a person had to be eighteen to buy a pregnancy test. That wasn't true, for the record, but that shows you how well prepared I was for the situation I was in. Anyway, lucky for me, I remembered that I'd seen an unopened box of pregnancy tests under the bathroom sink at home. I had no idea why there were there, but thank God. I couldn't wait another minute to face the music, and I wasn't in a state to figure out how to get one of my own.

It was only 2:30 when I finished school and got home to take care of business. I approached the whole task in robot mode. It was almost an out of body experience. No one knew I was taking a pregnancy test, or even suspected I was thinking about it. It was just me, alone, in the bathroom, with a little plastic stick that was about to turn my crazy gut feeling into an inescapable fact.

When the test was positive, it wasn't a big moment for me. It was just a formality, reality, confirming what had been obvious to me since I'd stepped out of the shower two days before. The test might as well have said, "Yep." So once that moment of anticlimax was over, I walked slowly out of the bathroom, down the hall, and into my bedroom to call Ryan. He was at work early that day, a good forty-five minutes away.

"Hello?" Ryan answered.

I knew he couldn't talk long, so I'd have to be clear and to the point. "It says it," I said.

There was a pause. "Hello?" Ryan said again.

"It says it," I repeated, only vaguely realizing that he hadn't been in my head for the last few days.

"What are you talking about?"

"I took a pregnancy test and it says I'm pregnant."

Whatever his response was, it was lost on me. For all my outward calm, I was a lot more dazed than I realized. The call was short. But I asked if I could come and see him at work, and he said yes.

Shifting into a quiet stealth-panic mode, I told my mom I was going to the mall with my friends. That was a completely unnecessary fib. She wouldn't have interrogated me or forbid me to go say hi to my boyfriend. But in my mind, I wasn't taking any chances. So I told her I'd be back soon, and I walked out the door without even waiting for her to respond.

Even more than taking the pregnancy test, the drive to Ryan's workplace felt completely unreal to me. It was almost like I was watching myself go through it. My emotions had run off somewhere to escape the reality that was taking shape. I don't even remember feeling anything, or thinking anything. I didn't cry. I didn't say much. I was just in complete, actual shock.

So was Ryan. He asked me the normal questions. Why didn't I tell him I was taking a pregnancy test? Was I sure? The look on his face was the definition of confusion. He just stared at me with big round eyes and tried to process what I was saying. It seemed hard for him to understand that something so big could happen without any kind of warning. After all, we'd only been together for about six months. We'd only been having sex for two. How could something like this come at us so fast? We were both reeling in disbelief, so it was quite an awkward conversation. And to top it off, he was still at work and could only stay outside for five or ten minutes before he had to get back on the job.

Finally we hugged and both tried to say the right things. We said our I love you's and told each other that we were going to be okay, that it would all be fine. It was obvious that every reassuring word coming out of our mouths was meant for ourselves as much as the other person. We may have prided ourselves on being low-drama types, but everyone has a threshold. No matter how chill you are, the words "I'm pregnant" can have a pretty powerful effect on your nerves. It went without saying that we were both freaking out inside.

That night, after everyone else in the house had gone to bed, I stayed up late in the den with the TV on and wondered what to do next. I did not want to tell anyone. My first reaction, even though I knew it didn't make realistic sense, was that it wasn't anyone else's business. But obviously I couldn't tell *no one*. That wouldn't really work.

I couldn't tell any of my friends something this serious. Not when I hadn't even wrapped my own head around it. They were my best friends and everything, but even then I was old enough to know that if you tell one fifteen-year-old a secret, she's going to have to pass it on to someone or it will drive her crazy. I didn't want it to get out of hand like that. Adding rumors and gossip to the mix could instantly turn the situation into a nightmare.

Finally, I decided to tell my brother Matt. Not only because he was one of my best friends, but because I knew he'd give me a real, valuable reaction that wasn't sugar-coated or overly negative. I felt confident that he'd listen to me and give me advice on what to do next, without getting angry at me or judging me. So I texted him from the den, woke him up, and told him I needed to talk to him. He didn't want to get up, but I told him it couldn't wait.

My brother and I sat there for about five minutes in silence while he waited for me to say whatever I had on my mind. But when he couldn't take it anymore, he asked, "What is it?"

I put my hand over my mouth like it would help filter the truth, and then I came clean. "I'm pregnant."

"I knew you were gonna say that," he replied, without missing a beat.

"How did you know?" I groaned. Great, I thought. So I have "PREGNANT" written on my forehead now.

"As soon as you said you needed to talk, I just knew it," he said. "Did you take a test?"

"Yeah. I took one."

"You need to take another one, just to be sure." And just like that, he stood up and told me we were going to the drugstore. Our dad noticed us leaving and texted us once we were out the door — we told him we were going out for a snack.

My brother went into the drugstore with me. We approached the checkout counter with three tests, and the woman working behind the counter told us they were more accurate when taken in the morning. We thanked her and headed back home.

"Try to get some sleep," he told me. "Take these in the morning before school, and come and tell me what they say."

I don't think I got any sleep that night. In the morning, I passed every one of those tests with flying colors. Meaning they all said I was pregnant.

I went to my brother's room. The door was ajar, so I knocked softly and pushed it open. "Are you awake?"

My brother was sitting up in bed and looked at me like, *Are you kidding?* "Do you actually think I've been asleep?" he asked.

"All the tests said I'm pregnant," I said. I felt nothing. I was still in shock.

"It's gonna be okay," my brother said, perfectly calm and reassuring.

"I don't know what I'm gonna tell them."

"Mom and Dad went through this themselves," he said. "They'll freak out, but they've been here before. It'll be okay and you know I'll always be here for you."

I hoped he was right. For the moment, all I could do was grab my stuff and head for school. Keeping my brother's support and confidence in mind helped me keep it together that day, especially once the shock wore off and my mind turned into an echo chamber of, "What the hell am I going to do?"

The first step I knew I wanted to take was going to the doctor. Even though I'd taken enough tests at that point to be sure I was pregnant, it still seemed smart to get an official confirmation from the doctor, just to be absolutely certain before I dropped the bomb with my parents. I also thought that if I could find a doctor, make an appointment, and get things figured out before I approached them, it would take some of the initial stress and burden off of their shoulders. Maybe they'd think, "Well, if she's done this all on her own, maybe she understands the seriousness of the situation and her responsibilities."

The trouble was I didn't know how to go about it. I was only sixteen, and I'd never even been to a gynecologist. Luckily, Matt had a friend who was pregnant at the time, and he asked me if he could tell her what was going on so she could give me some advice. Within the week, I'd called her doctor and made an appointment for two weeks away. But as soon as I hung up the phone, I thought, "Oh, no. I'm still a minor. What if they don't let me in without a parent?" When I called back to ask, they told me I could come in alone as long as I had my insurance information. I told them that was great, but really I was thinking, "Great. One more thing I don't know where to start with."

It was crazy. I hadn't even told my parents I was pregnant yet. I hadn't even been in a doctor's office. But already things were coming at me that were totally beyond my experience and understanding as a teenager. I got my insurance card from my mom by telling her I needed it for a job application. She found that odd, but she handed it over anyway.

When the appointment rolled around and I sat down in the waiting room with Ryan to fill out the paperwork, I had a fresh batch of problems. I'd never filled out my own medical paperwork before. The forms asked for information I had no clue about, along with my mom's social security number, since she was the insurance holder. I slunk back to the receptionist with the clipboard and told her I had no idea what anything meant. She walked me through it and helped me fill it out, and then it was time to see the doctor.

I'd been scared everyone was going to judge me at the doctor's office. I expected it to be really awkward. *You're sixteen, you're pregnant, you're screwed!* But it wasn't the case at all. The nurse who brought back my test result was as chipper as could be.

"You're definitely pregnant!" she told me with a big smile.

The doctor congratulated us right away, then asked us if our parents were looking forward to being grandparents.

Ryan and I looked at each other. "We haven't told them yet," I said.

The doctor didn't seem to pick up on my apprehension. "They're going to be so excited!"

"Well," I said, forcing a laugh. "Do you want to tell them for me?" Everyone was so friendly and excited, it was almost bugging me. I still hadn't figured out how to wrap my head around the situation all the way, so I didn't know how I felt yet. But I definitely wasn't feeling as festive as they were acting.

Then the doctor did an ultrasound, and time sort of stopped.

Ryan and I had no idea it was going to happen. But when we saw that little peanut on the screen and recognized the heartbeat, something incredible came over the room. The atmosphere in the room changed completely. Everything quieted down for that one peaceful, precious moment.

In that moment, everything became real.

Just like that, I felt all of the denial and bullshit dissolve from around my mind. In the middle of that scary, shocking time, that feeling of awe and amazement helped me put my feet on the ground. I thought, "You're pregnant. Here you go. This is your new life."

CHAPTER 4:

MY STORY STARTED DECADES AGO

my story started decades ago,
but life as i know it...
began when yours did.

a few days away from a few years,
i'm getting through what i got myself into.
all because of you, being beside me all the way.

all i had to offer you was my heart,
and from day one, that's all you ever wanted.
you are my heart.

this journey of growing up...
everything i learn i'll teach you,
as you are teaching me.

the chance to have a future,
i'll give to you.
because that's what you gave to me.

if i'm gifted a long life with you,
as your mother and friend.
my promise to you,
i will always love you more.

and when i'm gone,
if you learn anything from me...
i hope it's that you love yourself,
as much as i loved you.

CHAPTER 5:

SHOCKWAVES

My parents have been together since they were fifteen years old. My mom was sixteen when she got pregnant with my brother. But their story isn't a cautionary tale. They got married and stuck together, and they've been together now for almost thirty years. No matter how difficult things were, they worked as a team and managed to stay in love with each other all the while. No relationship is easy, but even when they fought, there was respect between them. You could always tell they still thought of each other as those two young people who fell in love back in high school.

I've always been close with my mom, and we were able to talk about anything. But that didn't mean we did talk about everything. Somehow, we never got around to talking about pregnancy and sex. To be perfectly honest, I think she just figured she didn't have to. It just so happens that my brother and I aren't half as rambunctious as our parents were when they were our age. When my mom and dad were teenagers, they were pretty wild. They ran with a rough crowd and partied hard. Not that they were total delinquents. Both of them had great parents and good morals. But my grandparents worked a lot, so there was plenty of time for a couple of fun-loving teenagers to get up to no good.

Compared to Mom and Dad, my brother and I were model citizens. And that was thanks to them. They always gave us enough freedom to be our own people, but they also kept an eye on what we were doing and who we were hanging out with.

They raised us to be smart and act right, and it seemed to be panning out just fine. They certainly had no idea I was having sex.

Ryan and I had never talked about pregnancy, birth control, STDs, or anything like that. We'd spent a lot of time talking about sex before we had it, but mainly we just talked about my virginity and whether it was a good idea for us to take that next step. When we finally slept together, protection never factored in. I have no idea why we thought that was okay.

I was aware of the risk, but it didn't seem as big, serious or real as it should have. On some irrational level, I felt disconnected from the idea of pregnancy. Part of it had to do with my own stereotypes about teen moms. It wasn't something I thought consciously about, but part of my carelessness was based on the feeling that I wasn't that type of girl. I wasn't a wild child. I didn't get into trouble. I'd waited to have sex, and I owned the decision. I wasn't a slut. Slacking off on condoms just didn't seem like a big deal.

And on a simpler level, I had no idea how to get condoms or birth control if I wanted them. In a way, maybe I just thought I could put off dealing with it. Breaking the rules for awhile in the meantime wouldn't be that big of a deal. How easy could it be to get pregnant?

Well, it turns out it was really easy to get pregnant. When I went to the doctor for the final pregnancy test, I'd been having sex for eight weeks. The test told us the pregnancy was eight weeks along. Later, we joked that we must have had a really good first night.

I hadn't been trying to hide anything from my parents. I could have been honest with my mom about losing my virginity to Ryan. I trusted her not to judge me. If I'd told her I was having sex, I'm sure she would have helped me figure out birth control. But she just never had a chance. My pregnancy would shock her, and I didn't know how to soften the blow. I had a horrible feeling there was nothing to do but get it over with.

The day after I saw the doctor, I came home from school determined to break the news. After she'd come home from work and gone into her office, I went in and made small talk about her day and mine. But whenever I saw a chance to come out and tell her I was pregnant, I just couldn't do it. I could feel the words in my mouth, and my lips just wouldn't let them out. Every time I tried, it was just silence. I couldn't do it.

At school the next day, it was hanging over me. Finally, while I was sitting in class completely unable to focus, I pulled my phone into my lap and wrote her a text.

"Mom?" I wrote.

"What?"

"I need to tell you something."

"I hate it when you do this," she replied immediately.

I couldn't remember ever having done that before, so I wasn't sure what she was talking about. It caught me off guard, and I didn't answer. After a few minutes I typed the words "I'm pregnant," but I didn't send the text. I just stared at it for about twenty minutes.

"Well?" my mom wrote.

I sent the text.

"What am I supposed to say to that?" she wrote back. "Oh shit, or haha?"

"I wasn't expecting either," I replied.

"If this is a joke, it isn't funny," she said. "If it's real, we'll talk when we get home."

"OK," I wrote, and got up from my desk. I didn't even ask the teacher for permission. I went into the bathroom and lost my mind, locking myself in a stall and bursting into tears. I wanted to look up the earliest flight to China, hop on, and never go home. I was freaking out. But then the bell rang, and I had to pull my shit together. My friends asked me if I was okay, and I told them I had something in my contacts.

As I was walking to my next class, I got a text from my dad asking, "Hey baby, are you okay?" I lost it again and ducked out of sight to write him back. I told him I was fine, and asked if he was okay. And he wrote, "Yes, I love you, and I'll talk to you later when you get home."

With that, I felt the first flicker of hope that it was going to be okay.

When I went home, my mom and dad were both waiting at the kitchen table. When I walked in, I just stood at the counter and said nothing at all. I didn't know what to do. But then my mom asked me to come and sit down. And as soon as I did, they both stood up and wrapped their arms around me, crying. I'd only seen my mom cry a few times in my whole life, and I'd never seen my dad shed a tear. It was a big deal for my family to have such an emotional moment. And while it was awful to see the concern in their eyes and not be in a position to reassure them, it was a huge relief to feel how much they loved me, and know that wasn't going to change.

Once we'd gotten hold of ourselves, we sat down and talked about everything that was going on. I told them about the past couple of weeks and my visit to the doctor. And I was surprised when my mom asked, "You're going to keep it, right?"

The question caught me off guard. "Of course," I told her, feeling almost offended. The way she'd asked made me feel like she was expecting me to say something else, and was all set to argue with me about it. But no other option had ever entered my mind. I told them Ryan knew and that he was as shocked as I was, but we were staying together.

My dad took a no-nonsense approach, as usual. He didn't sugarcoat anything. "This is your responsibility," he said. "We'll be here to help you and support you in any way that we can, but this is your child, and this is your job."

"I know," I said. "I know."

It was a little hard to be blown away by the message when I'd already had three weeks to think it over on my own. But then my dad said something I'd never forget. "You're going to be okay," he told me. "You'll be fine. You'll be able to do this. But it's going to be the hardest thing you've ever done, and the hardest thing you ever will do in your life."

"I know," I said again.

My father looked at me with tears in his eyes and said, "No, you don't." The look on his face was straightforward and dead serious, and he didn't have to tell me he was speaking from experience.

"Well," I said. "I don't know. But I'm just trying not to freak out and lose my mind."

With that, my dad had to go back to work. And that was kind of it. The cat was out of the bag, and it was full speed ahead.

Once that hard part was over, I shifted from shock to acceptance faster than I expected.

I've always been a "handle it" type of person. I try not to dwell on the negative or obsess over things I can't control. When a problem comes up, I try to solve it or deal with it. I don't like to complain or kick up a fuss when I run into an obstacle. If you sit around and think about how shitty things are, all that happens is that things stay shitty. I didn't have time for that. Why waste that energy? When life throws something unexpected in your path, the only useful thing to do is figure out how to get over, under, around or through it the best way you can.

All of this is easier said than done, of course, and I'd never been in a situation half as serious as the one I was in now. Even so, I only knew one way to handle it, and that was just to handle it. I didn't have time or energy to sit around feeling scared and sorry for myself. I was sixteen and I was going to have a baby. It wasn't what I'd planned, but that was the deal. I wasn't the first teenager to end up in this situation, and if anyone else could make it work, I could damn well do the same.

Even more importantly, as overwhelming as the situation was, I knew things could have been a lot worse. I had a caring family, a strong support system, good healthcare, and access to the resources I needed. I still had my relationship with Ryan, who had a steady job and a good family. I had a healthy environment and an army at my back, and these were privileges I quickly learned not to take for granted. I saw what it was like for teen moms who didn't have those basic advantages on their side, and the view was chilling. What would it be like to be sixteen and pregnant with no parental support, no stable housing, and no trustworthy adults to turn to for advice? That's exactly how it's been, and continues to be, for countless young women. But I was lucky. I didn't have any dark forces conspiring against me.

With my family on my side, it was time to step up to the plate. My situation was scary, but it wasn't more than I could handle. It couldn't be. No matter how scared or overwhelmed I felt, I knew I was capable of figuring it out. It was going to be a long, hard, rocky road, but I was on it, and it only led one way. So I just had to take the wheel.

CHAPTER 6:
SINK OR SWIM

You never understand how fast life can change until yours does. That spring, I might as well have gone to a different planet. That's how completely everything turned upside down. It had started without my knowledge the moment Ryan and I conceived a child, and by the time I started getting my ducks in a row, I was already on a one-way train racing toward a place I wasn't even remotely prepared to be in. I was going to be a damn mom!

I found out I was pregnant just in time for spring. Everyone was getting ready for summer, the last one before my senior year. When softball season kicked off, I got one of my first big reality checks. Senior year was going to be my last chance to really give softball my all, since I'd already decided I wouldn't be playing in college. But now that I was pregnant, there would be no more of that for me. It couldn't be helped, but by the same token, I couldn't help being disappointed. It was difficult not to say a real goodbye to the sport that had taken up half my life since I was four years old. All that year, whenever I heard any of the girls who were still on the team complaining about practice or not taking things seriously, it secretly drove me crazy. I would have given it my all until the last minute before I had to give it up. And to make it even more painful, the team went on to win state that year! That was a huge "damn it" moment.

My friends must have known I was upset, but they didn't get much out of me on the subject. Spring came and went before I made any sort of public announcement about my pregnancy. I even went to prom with all of my close friends and their boyfriends without giving it away. It wasn't until the last week of school that I started opening up about it. It wasn't that I was afraid of their reactions. I just didn't want to answer all of the questions. I was overwhelmed enough as it was without becoming an object of curiosity for the rest of the school year.

I told my best friend Sway first. We met in the parking lot after school so we could talk in private, and when she got there, I told her Ryan and I were going to have a baby. As I said it, I started to laugh a little, trying to cover up how nervous I was. Sway started to laugh, too, but her eyes filled up with tears at the same time. She didn't know how she was supposed to react, and I understood completely. There was a little bit of every emotion flying around. But later that night, she showed up with a stack of baby books she'd gone out and picked up.

After that, I went on to tell each of my closest friends, and everyone found out from there. Without fail, once the shock wore off, they were all supportive and showed tons of excitement. That's the thing about unplanned pregnancies. On one hand it can feel like a nightmare, especially for a teen with no concept of what's about to happen. But to conceive a child is such an awe-inspiring thing, and it's hard to be completely doom-and-gloom when you know there's a baby on the way. For me it was never as simple as just being scared, or just being excited. It was everything all at once.

And sometimes it was even nothing. The fact is, I don't remember much anxiety during my pregnancy. I don't remember being consumed by fear or nervousness. Not because I'd managed to achieve nirvana in my early teens, but because the best coping mechanism I could come up with was tunnel vision. Fear and uncertainty were always in the margins of my mind, darting around in my peripheral vision. But I knew that if I paid them any attention, they'd swarm in and take over. If I let those feelings in, I wouldn't be able to make things happen. In my mind, the only chance I had of getting my shit together was if I made myself bulletproof. I couldn't let fear get to me, or I'd fall apart.

So instead of focusing on fear, I focused on finishing the school year. My mom was a lifesaver. She was a big help in figuring out how to deal with the rest of my life. She took charge of my school arrangements, setting me up to graduate early through an accelerated program so I could finish up before my delivery date. And once that path was clear, she started in on preparing for the baby. I had no idea where to start, so she was the engine to my train. She guided me along with the doctors, the nursery, and everything along the way. By the time summer was in swing, my dad and brother had started to get excited, too. Especially once we found out the baby was a boy.

* * *

Ryan and I were doing fine. He proposed to me, and of course, I said yes. We made plans to move into an apartment together. Somehow my dad refrained from killing Ryan, and we started spending much more time with both of our parents. His family was great, although it was hard to wrap my head around having any kind of in-laws at the age of sixteen. But they stepped up right away to help us get ready for the baby. I spent a lot of time with his mom and my mom, working out all the details.

It didn't feel like my relationship with Ryan was in trouble. But it definitely wasn't the honeymoon phase anymore, either. There was a strange new distance between us as we both separately did what we had to do on the deadline we were on. Ryan got busy working and trying to save money, while I worked part-time for my dad and went to summer school so I could graduate early. Our schedules were suddenly very full, and they didn't include much time for each other. But that seemed like it was to be expected. If anything bugged me, it was that our attitudes about the whole thing didn't always seem to line up.

Sometimes when I brought up something about the baby, I got the feeling Ryan's brain just went somewhere else. And when it came to making actual plans for after the baby, whether it was work schedules or daycare, he was never in the mood to deal with it. It was all awkward silences, one-word answers, and impatient grunts whenever I tried to work out a vision of how we'd actually live once the baby arrived. And it was a good thing I wasn't expecting any special treatment while I was pregnant, because that wasn't happening. Sometimes I got the feeling he wanted to pretend there was no pregnancy, and we could go on acting like nothing had changed at all.

But there were times, too, when we joined forces like we were probably supposed to. We still met at Sonic whenever we had a chance before his shift started, and that was where we chose the baby's name. We were sitting in the parking lot with a baby name book, and at the time we didn't even know if we were having a boy or girl. But when we saw the name Bentley, we immediately knew that was what we wanted.

During fun moments like that, it felt like we were bonding over the pregnancy. And it was easy to chalk up the rest to how overwhelmed we were. I knew my brain was in overdrive, and I could only imagine he was going through the same thing. I wasn't in a frame of mind to step back and examine how we were doing as a couple, what we were missing and where we could do better at building or maintaining our relationship. At sixteen years old, I probably didn't have the emotional vocabulary for it, either.

But at the end of the day, I didn't have time to worry about me and Ryan. I figured we were both more concerned about Bentley. And anyway, we were engaged, and we were moving in together. That felt plenty solid.

For the most part, my tunnel vision seemed to be working out well. I was steady on my feet, and I didn't seem in danger of a nervous breakdown or anything. I'd barely even cried. But there was one moment when it all caught up to me, right when I was making the final move from home to the new place with Ryan. I'd just eaten dinner at my parents' house and I had my last few boxes in the car, because I was driving to the apartment for my first night there with Ryan. As soon as I drove off, I just lost it. I cried all the way there. I don't remember knowing exactly why I was so upset, whether it was because I was going to miss them or I was nervous or what. But I think somehow when I pulled out of that driveway, it finally became real that I was a grown-up — whether I wanted to be or not.

Living with Ryan wasn't difficult at all. For all of my being okay on my own, it's never bothered me to live with someone. After my moment in the car, I got over it and settled in for the final stretch.

* * *

Meanwhile, a funny thing happened. Since I was sixteen, pregnant, and didn't have a real job, my mom got the idea to look for maternity modeling opportunities for me. While she was browsing different listings on the internet, she came across a casting call for a new teen pregnancy documentary on MTV. Lo and behold, they were looking for people between the ages of fifteen and seventeen who were expecting a first child.

When she told me, my first response was "Absolutely not. I'm not going to be on TV because I'm sixteen and pregnant. That is not a good idea!"

"Well," she said, "they're gonna pay you, and you never know what it could turn out to be. You might as well write in. They probably won't even pick you."

Eventually I came around to the idea, enough to write in just a short introduction message. Just a week later, a woman from the casting department called me. I started wading in. Before I knew it, I'd had three different phone calls with this girl that lasted about three hours each. She wanted to know everything, from how many times per year I went to church to what my favorite car was. And when she'd had enough of that, she told me she'd be mailing me a flip cam and a sheet of questions for me to answer. Once that was done, it was off to the races. I just didn't know what that meant.

The show hadn't gotten the green light yet, so the producers were only showing up to film the pilot. At that point Ryan and I were already in the apartment together. Even though we all knew it was legit, my mom made my dad come over so he could be there when the producers arrived. "You never know!" she said, like there might be some criminal conspiracy afoot. But I didn't end up kidnapped. Instead, the producers sat in the living room with my dad and me and talked about what they had envisioned for this documentary.

Like most of the other girls on the show, I never imagined I was signing up to be part of some cultural phenomenon. Most of us thought it would be a one-off special, if anything, like the typical hour long TV documentary format featuring some random person with an interesting story. It didn't strike me as a long-term project, and I certainly didn't factor fame or fortune into my considerations. My big concern was that it would be done well. More specifically, that it wouldn't be scripted or fake. I appreciate good trashy TV as much as the next person, but I wasn't interested in becoming a reality TV personality. The only reason I considered the show was because it was conceived as a documentary series, not a reality TV drama. That made me feel a lot better. And after talking to my parents and the producers, I started to see more value in the idea. I thought that if by sharing my story I could help one teen girl get on birth control, or if some other pregnant girl out there could relate to me and wouldn't be so scared, it was a project worth taking on. So I signed the contract. We started filming, and then it got the green light.

Being the subject of a documentary is awkward at first, because you haven't gotten used to pretending the cameras aren't there. And at that time, I already felt like I was being stared at everywhere I went, on account of my being so young and so pregnant. Every time I went out in public I felt like everyone turned to look at the toddler having a baby. Adding a film crew on top just made it even crazier. But only for a little while. I got used to it, and it all felt normal very quickly.

Even after filming all of *16 & Pregnant*, I had no idea I'd hitched myself to a spaceship. I watched the show when it aired, but somehow I didn't make the connection that millions of other people were watching me right along with me. It was only when I went to the mall later that it hit me. People were approaching me and calling me by my name. They were asking for photos! Right away, the atmosphere told me it was much bigger than I ever thought it would be.

The show did a good job of representing me and my story. If there was one thing I wished might have been different, it was nothing they could have changed. It was just me and my personality. Watching the show, I saw the same calm, collected Maci everyone else did. The difference was that I remembered what was really going on inside my head at the time. Eventually, I started to understand how my introverted character became a double-edged sword on *16 & Pregnant* and *Teen Mom*. On one hand, I heard from countless teen moms who were going through the same thing I did, and who told me, "You're so strong, and you showed me that I could be strong. If you did it, I can do it."

On the other hand, there are many times when people say things like, "You make it look so easy. You're so put together. You make it look like you're not struggling at all." That's when I wish I'd broken down my walls a little more and shared my emotions on camera. I wished I could have shown people, especially younger girls, how much harder on me it was than it looked. I wished they could see that even for someone who kept it together like I did, had all the support that I did, being a teen mom was still the most difficult thing in the world. I wished I could make them understand that you can have the best family, all the best friends, and still feel like you're completely alone.

I almost never cry. Ever. Not in front of other people, and not when I'm alone. The list of things that can make me cry is very short. Either I'm extremely angry, or I'm worried about Bentley. Other than that, I'm just not a crier. It must be hereditary. Not only can I count the number of times I've seen either of my parents cry, but I don't know if I've ever seen them show that they were overwhelmed. I know they must have been, because everyone is at some point. And it's not as if we're not emotional people. But even though we're a very close family and very open with each other, we tend to keep our feelings to ourselves. I hardly ever fought with my parents as a teenager. My brother was the same way. They raised us to be very independent people, but I guess they earned so much of our respect we ended up a little dependent after all. Instead of rebelling, I ended up looking to them for answers and guidance. There were never any big blow-ups or stupid fights in our house. My parents kept things calm and respectful, and that's how we were raised.

In a way, that mindset made it impossible for me to deal with random drama. Instead of engaging with any craziness or passion, I ran from it. I didn't know what else to do! To be honest, I have no idea what my emotional outlet is. Maybe my parents did pass down some secret family gift for emotional regulation. Or maybe I'm just crazy. But if there's a simple explanation, it's that I really do make an effort not to let things get to me. It's the way I've always been, and if I can help it, it's the way I'll always be. I just believe, with every bit of my being, that most negative emotions are a waste of time and energy. Feelings like stress, fear, sadness, and jealousy happen to all of us, but they bring no solutions, and the cause is so often temporary anyway. Why let pointless negativity tear you apart if you can help it? There's almost always something more worthwhile you can distract yourself with.

Even though my philosophy didn't play exactly how I wanted for the cameras, it served me well the rest of the time. And it definitely helped keep me sane during my first pregnancy. It's not that I never got stressed. I just told myself, "It's okay. You're not gonna die if you don't get something done. It's all gonna get done. You know it will. Take it one step at a time. It's going to be okay."

CHAPTER 7:

5 WAYS TO SLOWLY KILL A RELATIONSHIP

1. Keeping all of your feelings to yourself.

I never wanted to be seen as being emotional or jealous or crazy. So if I was ever in a situation where I felt like something disrespectful or shady was going on, I didn't say anything because I didn't want to risk being accused of overreacting. But since I made no objections, the behavior continued and I just kept getting pissed off about it. The longer I held my silence, the harder it seemed to make a change, and the more resentful I felt.

2. Being disrespectful in private or public.

The way you treat each other in front of friends and family matters. You should never belittle another person, ever. But belittling your partner in front of friends or family is a sure-fire way to put your relationship on a downward trajectory. It makes the other person embarrassed and insecure, which leaves a resentment that's slow to fade. And it makes an impression on friends and family that you almost never get a chance to take back. Once your partner's friends and family turn against you, it's going to be very hard to have a healthy relationship.

3. Airing too much dirty laundry.

It's normal to vent to your friends about your relationship. But it's also easy to get carried away. Your friends and family care about how you're treated, and if you paint a negative picture in their eyes, it will be very difficult to erase. Even if your partner wins your forgiveness back, your friends and family will find it harder to move past what they heard. Worse yet, you might feel like you're being judged for putting up with all the things you said you couldn't stand.

4. Sex.

It can bring you closer together. But if you do it irresponsibly, it can also tear you apart. It's all fun and games until someone gets pregnant. Don't be stupid. Be careful!

5. Forgetting how to be friends.

Relationships are work, but they're not just work. It shouldn't feel like a constant stream of chores and problems. You have to be business partners, parenting partners, and sex partners, but you also have to be friends. Never forget how important it is just to like each other. Spend time bonding and making each other laugh. Always leave room for friendship between you. You can always still love somebody, but once you don't like them anymore, that's when you're in trouble.

CHAPTER 8:

PUPPY LOVE

Neither one of us did any sort of preparing for the actual delivery. At least, I could assume Ryan didn't. It was something neither one of us discussed. Chalk up another one for youth and ignorance, but we figured we'd know what to do when the time came. And in my case, I felt a weird stubbornness about it. I didn't ask for much advice, or read any books, or do any research or go to any classes. It would be hard to explain why. I felt like if I read ahead or went to classes or tried to feel prepared, I'd just be setting myself up for failure. I didn't want to lean on expectations based on other people's experiences. Basically, I didn't want to overthink it and set myself up to panic at the first surprise that popped up. Instead I wanted to trust my instincts and body rather than let my mind micromanage it.

Later I would think, "Holy crap. I can't believe I went through this at sixteen and decided to go in unprepared." What was I thinking? It's insane how much you change as you grow, and when I was older, I looked back and just shook my head in astonishment. I even wondered why no one ever took us by the shoulders and shook us. Why didn't they say, "You don't know it all and you don't have it together?" But at the same time, I was glad for my mindset. I knew that overanalyzing everything would just open me up to anxiety. It was better to go in with my confidence intact. That way I'd be stronger if anything came up and destroyed my expectations of how the experience would be. And I think the people who loved me sensed that. My parents knew what was best for me, just like I did. They knew I'd be able to handle it when the time came, and chose not to overwhelm me with doubts and warnings. The idea was to face it with confidence and an optimistic mindset and just go.

It was Saturday, October 25, and I had spent the night dressed up as a pregnant pirate for a Halloween party we'd thrown at the apartment. Ryan and I finally settled down to sleep, and not a second too soon. I was beat. I'd been running around all day doing all the usual hostess things, picking up decorations and getting the place ready for guests. That was probably what did it.

At about four in the morning, I snapped awake. It was pain that had woken me up, but by the time I came to, it was already just an echo in my mind. It wasn't even hard to fall back asleep. But not long after, I woke up again in the exact same way. Once again I could feel the pain fading just as fast as it woke me up. It was late, and I was sleepy, so I was completely without a clue. But the next time it happened, I hadn't quite drifted back to sleep yet. That was when I realized I was having a contraction.

I got out of bed without waking Ryan and went down the hall with my phone. Obviously, I called my mom.

"I think I'm having contractions," I told her. "What should I do?" She asked me what it felt like, and I described them and told her I thought they were about ten or fifteen minutes apart.

"Go and walk around," she said. "Take a shower and see if the same amount of time is happening between them, then call me back."

I went and did what she said, and the next ones were still between ten and fifteen minutes apart.

"Okay," she said. "When they get to be five minutes apart, call the doctor and then call me, and I'll come and take you there."

For the next forty minutes or so, I wandered around the house and felt the time between the contractions get shorter and shorter. Finally, when they were five minutes apart, I sighed and went back into the bedroom to wake up Ryan.

"I'm ready to go to the hospital," I said when he cracked his eyes open.

"Shit." Bless his heart, but he was hung over. Like, the dying kind. I couldn't help feeling bad waking him up that way at five in the morning, but it couldn't exactly be helped. "What?"

"I have to go to the hospital," I said again.

"Right now?" He blinked up at me like he was wondering if it was a nightmare. "Seriously?"

Somehow, we made it to the doctor, checked me in, and headed upstairs. When they came in to check my cervix, I thought things were well underway. But we weren't even close to getting started. Before being admitted to a room, my cervix had to be dilated to three centimeters. The pushing part of labor starts at ten centimeters. I was at two.

It didn't seem like a big deal at first. Nothing a good stroll around the hospital wouldn't fix. But after I'd walked around for awhile, it seemed I hadn't dilated any more. So to my complete and utter shock, they sent me home. I was not expecting that twist! Why was I going home when I was having contractions?

"Just go home," they told me. "Come back when the pain is so unbearable you can't even take it anymore. When you get there, we'll be ready."

"I am there!" I said. But it was no use. They wouldn't get started until my body said it was ready to go. So I got in my mom's car and went to my parents' house to wait it out.

The contractions kept coming, every few minutes, for the rest of the day. And the rest of the night. I didn't sleep. It was insanity.

I was in labor for twenty-four hours before I broke down and said, "We have to go back. I can't take any more." When I got back to the hospital, I was still only two and a half centimeters dilated. I thought I'd lose my mind if the show didn't get on the road. I walked a whole lap around the entire hospital, and then finally I hit the three centimeter mark and they let me get into a room. After that, things sped up. By the time the doctor came in to check me, I was at six centimeters.

"If you want an epidural, this is your chance," she said.

I had never planned to get an epidural. But I had been in labor for so long at that point, I was completely exhausted and over it. So I said, "Give me that."

The catch, of course, is that the epidural slowed things down. It was another four or five hours before the nurses came back in to find I was at ten centimeters. That was when the doctor said, "Okay, it's time to get everyone out. It's time to start pushing."

Whoosh. It was like all the air went out of the room for a second. My head started swimming. I looked at her like she had five heads and then just went blank, internally freaking out.

At that point I'd been in labor for over thirty hours, but it wasn't until she said it was time to push that I had a moment of flat out panic. It was almost like every scrap of uncertainty and fear I'd been holding back for the last seven months exploded like fireworks in my mind. "Hold on," I thought. "I need two more weeks. I'm not prepared for this. I don't know what I was thinking. This is not okay!" I don't think anyone knew, but inside I was freaking out.

It didn't matter, though. Things were happening fast, and it was time for me to push whether I was in a full-blown panic or not. I was so young and unprepared! When they said push, I went, "What do you mean, push? I don't know how to push!" That was when I just prayed my body would take over. I'd gone with the flow trusting my body to know what to do when the time came. And now I thought, "Okay, body, take over. Do it. I'm totally lost here." For a few moments I felt absolutely clueless, overwhelmed, and terrified. And then, thank God, it started to make sense. I started pushing.

When you've had an epidural you're still having contractions, but you can't feel them anymore. A machine beside you tracks when they're happening, and that's when everyone tells you to push. My contractions were just thirty or forty-five seconds apart. I had Ryan on one side and my mom on the other, and I started giving it my all. I pushed and pushed, every time another contraction took over, every half a minute. Contraction after contraction, minute after minute, until a half hour had gone by without any sense of progress whatsoever. At that point I felt like I had no idea what was going on. I didn't know how it was going anymore, and in a mix of exhaustion and my usual stubbornness, I wasn't about to ask.

But at the thirty-five minute mark, I was losing steam. I was so tired and drained that I started to drift off in the thirty seconds between contractions. Each time it was time to push, they had to wake me up. And I was so exhausted. Dead exhausted. It got to a point where I thought, "I can't do this anymore." I didn't feel it was physically possible for me to have this baby. There just wouldn't be enough left in me to pull it off. I had no idea what I was supposed to do, but it just wasn't working.

And then something weird happened. One of the monitors started beeping in an urgent way, and I heard a nurse say something about our temperatures rising. Bentley and I were getting a fever very suddenly, apparently. It wasn't clear, but the mood in the room shifted so plainly I could feel it even in my half-dead, delirious, exhausted state.

The doctor looked at me and said, "Okay. You get one more shot. One more chance to get him out, and that's it."

I didn't know what that meant, but I didn't even bother panicking. I saw her seriousness and told myself, "Okay. You can do it this time." And I just pushed. I poured everything into that last effort. I remember it took every ounce of will and strength I could find in me.

And then we had Bentley.

I never asked what happened or why things got tense, and no one ever brought it up with me. I knew they were worried, because as soon as Bentley came out, they took him over to the table to check him without even letting Ryan cut the cord. They were very impatient to make sure he was okay. But it all turned out fine. Bentley was healthy and crying, and everything was normal. They cleaned him off and measured him, and then, finally, they brought him over and put him in my arms.

"Oh my God," I said. "I actually had a really cute newborn."

It was the most teenager thing I could have possibly said at that moment, but at least it came from the heart. And he wasn't just cute. He was absolutely perfect.

* * *

The best word to describe my first days of motherhood is "surreal." The hospital experience became a blur in my memory. It was a hectic event. There were sixty people in the waiting room, plus camera crews from MTV. I'd been in labor for thirty-seven hours. I'd barely slept. Plus, I was still completely clueless as to how to care for a child. And yet somehow in the midst of all that chaos, I felt completely at peace. I'm talking Zen-like bliss. Maybe it was just my psychological reaction to the chaos, my way of not succumbing to how overwhelmed I really felt, but I felt like I just had a little oasis of calm in the middle of everything. Like I said, it was surreal. Nothing in the world could ever compare to the way it felt. There's no experience that will ever measure up to that.

The euphoria caught me completely off guard. When people talk about being new parents, they always seem to jump right to the difficult parts. It's always jokes about forgetting what sleep is, or what free time is, or what peace and quiet is. I was braced for all of that. And when I was pregnant, I wasn't really the type to sing lullabies to my belly. Some women seem to have a kind of mystical experience during pregnancy where they feel intensely bonded with the child growing inside of them. I was more perplexed by the experience. In the later months when I could lie in bed and watch my belly move, I'd just laugh. I always joked, "Until it comes out and it's a human baby, it's just a cute little alien." I didn't have a special, glowing feeling about pregnancy. More like my back hurt.

So with that attitude going in, I was totally unprepared for the sudden, enormous, completely pure love that consumed me when I held Bentley in my arms for the first time. It was just instant, automatic, life-changing love. And it was a mind-blowing feeling, especially considering that all newborns really do is cry, poop, spill things, and take all of your energy. But I felt that bond strongly and immediately. It made the entire experience so enjoyable.

Everyone warned me that parenting was exhausting and hard, and it's true that all babies really do is cry, poop, spill things, and take all of your energy. Everyone told me that it's exhausting and draining and very difficult and a lot of work. But no one told me that I would want to do it. I didn't know it would give me so much pleasure to get up out of bed when he was crying and pick him up and make him feel better.

Those first weeks played like one happy scene in my head. Waking up in the middle of the night I would hear him fussing in his bassinet and even though I could hardly hold my eyes open, I would get up and go straight to him. It was so rewarding to be the person who could make him feel better, or fix what he wanted. I would lie in bed with him, dozing off but resisting at the same time, just appreciating the moments, even when I was absolutely exhausted. Times during the day when my mom would be doing chores and my dad would be around doing something, and I'd lie on the couch feeding Bentley, feeling like it was just me and him and feeling very complete.

Ryan was really proud and overwhelmed at the birth. At the same time, I could tell he was shocked by the reality of the responsibility that came with it. When that excitement and shock wore off, he just looked completely lost.

I was lost, too, but I was too happy to mind. The haze of contentment and love I was drifting in for the weeks after Bentley's birth seemed to prove I had managed to adapt, after all. It's so interesting how smart our bodies are, and their ability to do what they need to do when they need to do it. That became clear to me during labor, delivery, and the first weeks of Bentley being home. I hadn't prepared. I didn't know what I was doing. My only points of reference were movies and TV. But even though my mind had no idea, my body and instincts took over without me having to reason anything out. That was amazing to me, and I loved it because it gave my mind a level of freedom I hadn't expected. By letting my maternal instincts take over, I could let my mind soak up the amazing experience I was having.

The first night in the hospital, when he would cry, I didn't know what to do or what he was crying for. At first I was freaking out. But I learned quickly that I could understand what he was crying for. It was as if, because I was his mom, I could communicate with him almost intuitively. When others were in the room and he started to cry, I watched them go through the checklist: "He just ate, so he can't be hungry. He just had his diaper changed, so that's not why." But for me, his cry told me exactly what he needed. I would know immediately.

In some ways, the experience of motherhood left me in awe. In a weird way, it helped me to understand the basic nature of human beings, how strong our instincts are, and the fact that we're animals. Intellectually I would expect to struggle with things, but when my baby needed me to do something, my body and instincts just obeyed. It amazed me to witness that within myself.

I don't know if fathers have the same innate tendencies that moms do when babies are born. My only experience was as half of a very young couple. I don't know if it's different for fathers who are older and more grown up inside and out. They say women mature younger than men. Maybe men develop nurturing instincts later in life. But I don't think it's common for young fathers to feel the same automatic, intense attachment to a newborn child as it is for young mothers.

The first flicker of warning was in the hospital that first night. I didn't let the nurses take Bentley to the nursery. That was stubborn of me! I went on to share that lesson with future parents: Let them take the baby! Get as much sleep as you can! But at the time, I didn't want to let him out of my sight. And that night, as I was drifting off to sleep, I realized I'd made a terrible mistake. Bentley was crying, and I didn't know what to do.

I'd been in labor for thirty-seven hours. Thirty-seven hours of pain and fatigue with no break, no sleep. I'd been talking to all of these people at the hospital. I was exhausted beyond anything I'd ever imagined.

Ryan was sleeping across the room. And as I lay there kind of freaking out, I expected, or hoped, he'd get up to do something to help. But he was just sleeping through it and not at all worried about anything but continuing to sleep. And there was a moment when I thought, "What in the world? I need you to get up and help me, what are you doing?"

But being me, I said nothing. God forbid anyone should know I was struggling a bit. My mind and body were so wiped out I couldn't even imagine feeling rested again, but the baby was crying and his father, somehow, was going to sleep right through it. I didn't know if it was that motherhood instinct that kept me from passing out cold or if it was just sheer force of will, but either way, I handled it.

CHAPTER 9:

CHANGE OF HEART

For the first few weeks, there was no clear picture of how our family life would be. For one thing, it was all incredibly new and exciting. For another, we had our moms there helping us. My mom stayed with us for a week, and then his mom stayed with us for a week. They were an enormous help. Without them I would have had a much harder transition into the difficulties you have to get used to as a mom. And I was as in the dark as Ryan when Bentley was born. I had never changed a diaper or fed a child. I wasn't even a big fan of kids, to be honest. But I managed to adapt to my role and rejoice in it. It wasn't like everything was perfect and fun all the time. Changing diapers isn't a hobby. But as a mom, I found there was intense satisfaction in knowing that I was the one who calmed down my baby and made him feel better. There was a deep feeling of reassurance in that. It steadied me to know that I was providing someone with that feeling of peace.

Young dads may not have the same instinct. I couldn't guess either way. There's a commonplace attitude that they just aren't as driven to nurture as women are. And maybe science can back up that theory someday. But in the meantime, in the real context of parenting, those low expectations can sometimes seem like a convenient cop-out. There are plenty of men with children who are good fathers and don't seem so agonized by a lack of parental instinct. It doesn't matter, anyway, whether they feel the same internal drive that mothers do. They can still invest in the family, and keep investing in their relationship. If a father doesn't have the same automatic natural feelings about parenthood, he can still be willing to help. Because even if the mother might be more instinctively compelled to jump out of bed automatically when the baby cries, that doesn't mean she doesn't get just as tired as anyone else. Nothing stops any father from taking on his fair share of the responsibilities, and even learning how to find satisfaction in it.

After our moms left and things slowed down, it was just me, Ryan, and Bentley at the apartment. Almost right away, I knew that I was going to be kind of on my own in the whole parenting thing. Ryan was a provider in the sense that he went to work every day and paid the bills. But I was getting up with Bentley every single time in the middle of the night and every single morning. Meanwhile, it seemed like Ryan always had some sort of reason not to be in the house. If he wasn't at work, he was at the gym or at dinner with friends, and by the time he made it home, he would just go right back to sleep without even spending time with Bentley.

I didn't know if he was overwhelmed by the thought of figuring out what to do, or if he just wasn't interested. Maybe he was afraid of messing up, so he decided not to try. Or maybe it was because I wasn't asking for help, so he thought I didn't need it. And it was true that I didn't express my frustration to him when I could have. But I didn't want to be that person. It was just a bad mixture brewing between young parents.

Once the hustle and bustle following the birth had faded, Bentley was my only company. My friends were making their ways through senior year. My parents had stepped back to let me settle into motherhood. And Ryan was always working or doing his thing. Slowly but surely, unhappy feelings began to creep in. For one thing, I was no longer quite as okay with that whole concept of being on my own. It was great when I was just a typical teenage girl with a healthy sense of independence. But now I was a teen mom in an adult life with a fiancé and a baby, and I couldn't make it all work by myself. I needed support, communication, and company. I believed that Bentley needed a good relationship with his father. And when the reality of what was really happening snapped into place, it felt like my wheels spun out.

From that first moment in the shower when I knew I was pregnant to the moment Bentley was born, a million fears and doubts circled the edges of my mind. But I never thought I'd be raising Bentley without a father. We were engaged. We lived together. We had our families supporting us, our moms helping us, our friends excited for us. And we had this amazing child who needed us both to be there with him. It wasn't just that our circumstances could have been worse. We didn't even have it that bad. We actually had it pretty good. There was no reason for me to think we wouldn't be able to make it work and be happy as a family.

* * *

While things between Ryan and me looked worse by the week, things between Bentley and me were great. I got lucky. Bentley was really chill. Apart from when he was being a normal newborn, needing a bottle every three hours and crying when he didn't get what he wanted, he was never a big whiner. In fact, he showed no interest in any of the usual baby quirks that drive new parents crazy. He never had tummy aches. He liked the first formula I gave him. No allergic reactions to soaps or laundry detergents. Even his teething phase barely made an impression on my memory, because somehow it never drove him to the kind of meltdowns you're taught to expect.

People make a big deal out of a baby's first words. For me the big moment was when he started cooing. For a month or so, babies don't really make any noise except for crying. So when you catch them making their first attempts at the kinds of sounds that will someday turn into words, it's almost mind-blowing. There was something so amazing to me about watching him go through those first increments of growing and developing. I could look into his eyes and see his little brain starting to work things out. I'd talk to him, and he'd reply to me with his little sounds. It was so incredible and sweet. I could actually see him transforming from a crazy baby to a real person. That had more of an impact on me than his first words did. There was a lot of wonder involved in parenting. It was fascinating in all of these ways I hadn't expected. I loved watching him pick up on things. It's so interesting to watch them learn the most basic things from scratch, just through instinct and adaptation.

And yet for all the wonder and whimsy in the house, the tension between Ryan and me was still just creeping deeper and deeper. To my complete shock and confusion, I just couldn't figure out how to share that joy and excitement with him. Bentley was like this amazing, special energy in the house that was so easy to tap into. But I just couldn't seem to get his father to see the appeal. And each day he found a reason he couldn't spend time at home, I started grappling with the ugly possibility that he just didn't want to be there.

If I was honest with myself, the doubts had started to creep in during the pregnancy. I wasn't blind. I'd seen the hints of disinterest and the gap between our attitudes toward the baby and about what would happen next. But at the time, I had no idea what to do other than to wait for the craziness to die down and then get to working on it. I didn't know what to do when it got worse. And it really did.

We started arguing all the time. If we weren't arguing, we weren't around each other. And I know my personality was part of the problem in that I didn't want to ask him for help. I still didn't consider myself that type of person. I wanted to be strong and composed and calm. Even though I needed him, I didn't know how to let him know without sounding needy or weak. And frankly, I never thought I would have to spell it out. Forget about whether or not I could expect him to love parenthood as much as I did. There was a baby in the house. It was our baby. We were his parents. There were obvious things that needed to be done, and it was way too much to expect one person to handle.

I could have said that outright. But I didn't. And maybe that was why he seemed to think it didn't matter if he was around or not. Maybe he just didn't know what to do, or he was afraid of screwing up, so he decided not to try. Maybe that was what fueled the distance between him and me and Bentley. It was possible. Unfortunately, we were both people who didn't express our emotions freely. We didn't communicate as well as we should have, and if that didn't make it worse, it definitely didn't make it better.

My parents had stayed together when they'd been in this situation. I thought Ryan and I could do the same. We were struggling, but they'd struggled, too. They had made it, so there was no reason we couldn't come out the other end. It seemed simple enough to me. If anybody else could do it, couldn't we do it? Wasn't that obvious? It didn't matter. I started to worry that I'd pushed all the fear and negative emotions aside for so long, I hadn't been entirely realistic with myself. I wasn't prepared for how much of a change having a baby was. I wasn't ready to see it cause such an ugly reaction. Certainly not from the father.

There were a few months after Bentley was born and things had gone south where we had both acknowledged we weren't in a good relationship, but we agreed we were going to work it out for Bentley. Unfortunately, things never got better. Eventually there wasn't even enough of a connection for us to rescue. If we had still felt a bond and were still in love, I could have fixed things he didn't like and he could have fixed things I didn't like. But there was no mutual desire to build on.

It got to the point where I didn't recognize our relationship anymore. I didn't recognize him. He seemed to be a completely different person. And I had changed, too, drastically. Both of our lives had changed drastically. But no matter what, I was still Maci. Where had Ryan gone? Where was the nice, easygoing, courteous guy who'd shown so much respect and interest? I didn't understand what had fundamentally changed between us, or within him. But we were miserable together. And when Bentley was asleep and I sat down on the couch to zone out in front of the TV, I felt so alone. It started to settle in: Now it's just you and this baby, and you don't have anyone else.

Whatever Bentley was doing, I was doing. I'd wake up and feed him, watch TV, and we'd just sit around. Babies sleep a lot. So it was just days full of feeding him and watching TV. I tried not to let myself get really depressed about it, but it was very, very lonely. Even when I did manage to see my friends once in awhile and hang out and do things, I just felt lonely. I had no one to share my experience with. I had someone I was supposed to share it with, but he was always somewhere else. There were times when I just sat there at night and thought to myself, "How did you get here? Why is this happening?"

I had no idea how things had gotten so toxic. But it was getting to be time to face the facts and deal with it. There was no getting around it: Something had to give. I got to a point where it was bouncing back and forth in my head. It was awful. I could either leave and be out of it and not have to deal with it anymore. Or, I could accept that this was just how it was, and hope that it would get better, hope that maybe when Bentley was older, his father would be more emotionally available. I didn't want to give up. I didn't consider failure an option. I didn't want Bentley to have parents who weren't together. I didn't think that it was serious enough for me to leave, but I also worried that I'd lost perspective.

We were just miserable together. We fought, and that was it. That was literally it. That environment wasn't good for me, or him, or anyone. It wouldn't be good for Bentley in the long run. Pretty soon I went from not wanting Bentley to have separated parents, to not wanting Bentley to have parents who argued all the time. And on a different level, I knew I could do better for myself, too. It got to a point where I thought to myself, "You can't live like this forever. This isn't you. You're not going to settle for this."

A failing relationship is the kind of weight that builds up so gradually you don't even notice it until it's completely dragging you down. It's almost an unpleasant shock to lose that burden, as freeing as it is. Giving up on that relationship was a difficult decision. It was the first point in my life when I realized that no matter how hard I worked, things weren't always going to go the way that I had planned them. I had to swallow my pride and accept it.

In December, when Bentley was a little more than a year old, Ryan and I finally called it quits.

* * *

Maybe if Ryan and I had communicated better, it could have worked. But I came to believe that we wouldn't have lasted anyway. The most we could have hoped for was to keep it alive longer, patching it up and dragging it along until there wasn't even a dead horse left to beat. But in fact, it felt like we'd done that already. Even if we had turned around and started doing everything perfectly, there was no love left to back it up. We had grown too far apart, and we didn't like each other anymore. I did miss the person I knew before everything changed, and it was hard for me to understand how we went from being so in love and obsessed with each other to literally hating each other. But I'd almost forgotten what the good times were like. All I knew was misery with him, and I'm sure that was all he knew with me, too.

At first, before it all sank in, there was a huge sense of relief when that weight fell from my shoulders. It was time for the next chapter. The sun was shining and the air was fresh. But that happiness didn't last for long. A few days later, I started to feel uncertain about the whole thing. Maybe I didn't believe we would be broken up forever. A part of me hoped that the breakup would jar him into realizing what he was giving up. I hoped he would miss me and want us to be back together. I hoped he would realize he wanted to be a part of Bentley's life and start to make it happen. So I wasn't happy when I saw him move on as quickly as he did.

Then, of course, I started to hear things. About the girls he had been talking to, and the places he'd been. I didn't seek the information out, but I didn't have to. Sometimes when you break up with someone, that stuff starts to trickle into your hearing range whether you want it to or not. There were many things I heard that I didn't care to hear. I wasn't shocked, but it wasn't fun.

Still, I knew I'd made the right decision. Life didn't get easier in general, but I was glad to lose at least one painful problem. The biggest improvement that came out of the breakup was not having to fight anymore. Not just in terms of arguing with him, but in terms of pouring so much of my energy into saving a doomed relationship. I didn't have to worry about what he was doing anymore. I didn't have to worry about asking him for help and dealing with his anger. I didn't have to worry if we got along at all. I was glad to be back in the light after spending so long in that tunnel of anger and sadness.

But the bad stuff didn't all disappear. Some of it just evolved. Even though he and I were completely over each other, we were still connected in one obvious way. Because we had a child together, there was no chance of having a normal breakup, closing the book and never looking back. We would still have to talk about Bentley and where he'd be each day, or, as it turned out, each weekend. Even after breaking up, that was one huge argument that refused to die. When I thought Bentley was going to visit his father for the weekend, I would sometimes make my own plans to visit friends or have a night or two to myself. But when I'd take Bentley to his grandparents' house, his father was never there.

It was infuriating for two reasons. First, because Ryan wasn't appreciating the chance to spend time with him. Second, because that left me feeling guilty about doing my own thing. If Bentley was supposed to be with his dad and then his dad didn't show, it didn't feel right to just leave the little guy in the care of his grandparents. And it hurt to see him being stood up over and over. The only comfort was that he was too young to realize it. But it drove me crazy to see the days going by, Bentley getting older and growing up, and no progress being made in his relationship with his father. I couldn't understand what I was witnessing.

I tried not to fight what I couldn't change, but I felt so helpless and frustrated at times I wanted to rip my hair out. That was the hardest part of the breakup. I'd withdrawn myself from the relationship, but Bentley couldn't. And so Bentley's father's bad behavior didn't affect me on a relationship level anymore, but it hit me on a protective parenting level. That turned out to be way worse.

I wasn't afraid of being single. But I was afraid of being on the journey of parenthood alone and the battle that it was sure to become. And for the first time in my life, I found myself horribly lonely. I was supposed to be good at letting go of negative feelings, but it wasn't as easy to distract myself anymore. If I'd been a "normal" eighteen year old girl, I would have called up some friends to go out and do something. But I had a kid to take care of. I couldn't just go out every weekend or random nights and have fun all the time. And I accepted that. I still enjoyed being a mom, and I loved being around Bentley more than anything. But your baby can't be your only company, and when he was asleep, I was on my own with the TV again.

What was I going to do? I didn't want Ryan back, and I wasn't desperate for the next romance. It wasn't about that. It was my feeling of being isolated from the rest of the world, like this new life of mine was taking place on a deserted island. Sometimes those lonely nights seemed endless.

CHAPTER 10:

THIS YEAR HAS BEEN A TEST

this year has been a test for me
and through all the times of betrayal
i lost the person i used to be

i sold her to the people around
because my effort was spent on loyalty
maybe i let her run away

i miss the girl i used to be
or maybe i forgot to please her
in the midst of all the royalty

everything i have to give is gone
is this the payback i'm supposed to see
but what if i'm not to blame

i don't know who i'm supposed to be
was i supposed to fall apart like this
without a root there is no tree

CHAPTER 11:

DISTANCE MAKES THE HEART GROW FONDER

When friends and family heard I was single again, they were surprised by the suddenness of it. Or, at least, what might have seemed like suddenness from the outside. But they could not have been all that shocked. No one tried to talk me into working things out with him. No one said much of anything, really. Probably because, as usual, I didn't say much about it either.

Despite the cloud of loneliness that was hanging over the back of my mind in general, I was glad to be single. It wasn't like I'd totally lost the strength I'd always felt in being alone. And as an eighteen-year-old mom with no idea of what to do next, I could definitely benefit from having the space to think for myself and focus on stabilizing my life.

Before I got pregnant I'd planned on culinary school, but so much for that. One of the first things anyone in the restaurant industry tells you is that it's impossible to establish yourself without dedicating loads of time to work. It's a notoriously difficult career to balance with a family life, and so it was out of the question for me. I wasn't going to devote all my nights and weekends to work now that I had Bentley. It was that simple.

With that plan off the menu, I wasn't sure what I really wanted do next in terms of a career. But I felt a strong desire to take forward steps, so back when Ryan and I were still together, I enrolled in college for a general business degree. I had particular passion for business. I was just doing it because that's what I thought I was supposed to do. And everyone knows that if you don't know what to study, that's the one to go for.

I spent my first semester on campus. I went to school, showed up for class, then went home and did homework. It wasn't exciting. It wasn't like I wanted to be there, and I wasn't taking classes I enjoyed. I was just going and taking my requisites, then going home. My mom had started working from home so she could take care of Bentley while I was at school. I felt bad about it. I knew it wasn't her responsibility to care for my child all day while she was doing her work, too. I felt like I was pawning him off on her. And frankly, I hated being away from him. At the same time, I was generally exhausted from being up all night with him. With my complete lack of interest and enthusiasm for school, my fatigue, and my desire to be with Bentley, it was only a matter of time before the whole college effort fizzled. After a month and a half I dropped my classes to avoid failing.

I knew I would go back to school, but I wanted to find something I was interested in before I tried to go back. Instead of going to class, I spent that spring and summer working for my dad and taking care of Bentley. Most of my days consisted of spending time with my baby, doing nothing. After awhile, I started to feel like a loser for dropping out. I criticized myself for the decision, wondering if I hadn't tried hard enough, if I was just making excuses. A baby is a lot of work, but you can still accomplish things. Knowing how important it was to get a degree, I should have stuck it out. I was claiming I was busy, but I could have done online courses from home. And I had the privilege of working for my dad and having control over my schedule.

But emotionally, and mentally, I just wasn't there. I was overwhelmed by everything I'd gone through since I found out I was pregnant. There was no way for me to succeed in school when I wasn't able to mentally check in. So I settled into a safer routine. It was all I could do until I came up with a better plan.

* * *

Before I met Ryan, I was happy without a boyfriend. I enjoyed being on my own and avoiding the drama that came with relationships. But my sense of independence was only part of the story. It's possible that my lack of interest in romance may have been influenced by a relationship I already had in my life. And once again, it had something to do with motocross.

My brother and I grew up riding dirt bikes and racing, although he was much more serious about it than I was. The more serious you are about racing and competing, the more you have to travel. Most people who show real talent for racing, and have the means to pursue it, are homeschooled from middle school onward. There's no other way to get an education when you're always on the road, traveling from state to state to compete. All of this plays into the culture surrounding motocross, by the way, and the kind of people who are drawn to it.

Back when I was about nine and my brother was in his early teens, our family spent a lot of time at the motocross tracks in and around Tennessee. Over time, my parents made friends with a few other families that were always at the same tracks. They were always around each other and hanging out. One of the boys my brother hit it off with was a guy named Kyle. I saw a lot of him when I was a kid. Of course, we weren't friends. He was my brother's friend, and I was just "Matt's little sister." As we all got older, my brother and I both got heavily involved in school sports. I was totally committed to softball, and he was serious about wrestling. Eventually he quit racing, and we all stopped spending so much time at the track. We still saw Kyle and the rest of the motocross people once in awhile, but not nearly as much.

One day when I was in high school, Kyle and I started chatting on MySpace out of the blue. I never had anything but a friendly impression of him, so I was happy to talk to him and catch up on what we'd been up to since I stopped coming to the track so much. The small talk led to more talk, and before I knew it we were becoming really good friends. Long-distance friends, but still.

After I'd been talking to Kyle for a few weeks, I brought him up with my brother. "Do you remember Kyle?" I asked him, very casually.

"Yeah, I remember." My brother gave me a weird look. "We basically grew up with him."

Right. "Is he cool?" I asked. "Or is he a douchebag?"

My brother laughed. He knew exactly what I was talking about. The money-and-homeschool combination that's common with serious motocross kids doesn't always result in the best personalities. It's a well known stereotype of people who grow up deep in that world that they basically know nothing about life. But my brother said, "He's cool. He's not a 'bro.'"

It was good to hear, but I already knew that. It wasn't like I was short on good friends, even guy friends. If I didn't see something cool about Kyle, I wouldn't get so much out of our conversations. But I loved talking to him. Kyle was really funny. He had a sharp wit, and not a mean one. He was the type of person who was always in a good mood. It was a strange relationship we had, spending so much time together on MySpace and on the phone, but he became my best friend.

Still, even though neither of us referred to it outright, the "friendship" between Kyle and me quickly turned into a kind of long-distance romance. Or at least it would be hard to explain how that wasn't basically what we were doing, at least in teenager terms. We talked all day, every day. And I mean constantly. Obviously neither one of us was spending significant time with other people in that way, considering the amount of attention we were paying each other. And so it wouldn't be a stretch to assume that part of the reason I wasn't interested in dating was because Kyle's friendship was already satisfying any need I might have had for a close connection with a guy I liked.

The fact that neither of us came out and labeled it as romantic was part of the appeal. In fact, what I had with Kyle was perfect for my personality and the way I liked to go about my life at that time. It was easy. Since he lived in Nashville and we never saw each other, getting physical wasn't an issue. Not that I didn't find him attractive, but I was younger then, and any relationship between a girl and a guy is simpler when sex isn't a factor. Not seeing each other also meant that we never had a chance to get on each other's nerves. Since we never crossed the line into girlfriend and boyfriend territory, we didn't even have to play the usual silly teenage relationship games like "you didn't text me between classes so I'm not talking to you," or whatever else couples usually harassed each other about.

I also liked the fact that what I had with him was completely my business. I didn't know anyone he knew, and he didn't know anyone I knew. Nobody had to know about us talking, and since I wasn't exactly a chatterbox when it came to my personal life, nobody really did know. I got to enjoy the best parts of dating someone without having to be the subject of any high school dating gossip. We had each other's company when we wanted, but out in the open it didn't exist. And by the same token, that made me feel freer to open up with him. In a way, our relationship felt kind of like a sanctuary from the people and places in my everyday life. I was comfortable sharing things with him that I'd normally keep to myself. Not that I had any thoughts in particular that required me to lead a double life. It was just that the long-distance arrangement made it easy for me to trust Kyle as a confidant.

But, again, we weren't exactly a couple. We resisted taking that step for so long that we got comfortable right underneath it. After that we were too afraid to try being girlfriend and boyfriend because we didn't want to mess with the amazing friendship we had. Which meant neither of us was in a position to do or say anything to stop each other from dating other people. So nothing stopped me from meeting Ryan and giving him a chance to win me over. And once he did, my close friendship with Kyle quickly dropped down a few notches in intensity.

Kyle wasn't very happy about it. We kept talking after I met Ryan, and I was always open with him, so he knew what was going on. He was definitely jealous of Ryan, but he couldn't do anything about it. That's the problem with the gray area we'd enjoyed so much up until that point. When Ryan and I got serious, it kind of pissed Kyle off. I was sorry about it, but at the same time, I knew that if I wanted to make a relationship work with Ryan, I was going to have to stop talking to Kyle. It wouldn't have been appropriate or even possible for our friendship to stay like it was. The simple fact was that Ryan and I were in love and I no longer had space for an almost-romance with someone else. So I took a big step back, and just like that, Kyle went back to being a friend of mine in Nashville.

I was about five months pregnant when I finished junior year, and it was starting to show. That was when I started telling everyone I was going to have a baby. But Nashville hadn't gotten the news yet. Just after summer vacation started, Kyle texted me out of the blue to say he missed me. But the way he referred to me and Ryan was more spot on than he probably would have liked. "You never talk to me anymore," he complained. "Pretty soon you're going to be married with kids or something."

That was either funny or it wasn't. It was hard to say. But at the time I rolled with it. "Yeah," I replied. "To be honest, I already am."

"WHAT?"

Kyle had known I was a virgin. We'd discussed it, though not in a flirtatious way. There just wasn't much we hadn't discussed. But since I stopped talking to Kyle when Ryan and I got serious, he obviously had no idea I'd lost my virginity. He definitely wasn't prepared to find out I'd gotten engaged and pregnant since the last time I talked to him. I didn't expect him to be happy about it, and he wasn't. We didn't speak again at all.

* * *

When Bentley was about four or five months old, I made plans to go to a Supercross race that happens every February in Atlanta. I knew Kyle would be there, so I reached out and asked him if he wanted to meet and catch up. I missed having him to talk to. It was almost painful sometimes not having someone to talk to the way I used to talk to him. I'd never needed that sanctuary so bad. Ryan and I were going south fast. I hadn't given up on us yet. At that point, I was completely determined to save our relationship. But I kept failing, and I was miserable. I felt like I was lost in the weeds, not knowing what to do about anything, and I was too stubborn to turn to anyone around me for help. And apart from all that, I had never wanted to lose Kyle's friendship completely. I missed him, and if there was a way to talk to him again, I knew I'd be glad.

I was right. Kyle and I picked up right where we left off, except that there was no more flirting or blurred lines. It annoyed him that Ryan had gotten in between us, but he welcomed me back as a friend and had no expectation that we'd be exactly the way we were before. We started talking again. He asked me what was going on, and I told him. In that sense, it was just like before. I opened up and confessed everything I'd been dealing with, including what was going on with Ryan and how hard I'd been struggling to get him to take an interest in Bentley and me as a family. As usual, Kyle didn't try to make assumptions or tell me what I should do. He was just there to listen.

Even when things got really bad and I was a total downer about my state of affairs, Kyle was always good about not judging me or showing any sort of irritation. I appreciated that. Having been on the other side of conversations with friends who complain and complain and talk about ending relationships but never actually do it, I knew how annoying it was to listen to. But Kyle was as patient and supportive as ever when I needed to vent.

Like most people, Kyle was less than shocked when Ryan and I broke up. To be honest, his reaction was fairly subdued. After hearing so many reports from the roller coaster, he probably thought we were just going to get back together. But once the dust had settled and it was clear that the case was closed, it wasn't long before Kyle and I got back to our old flirtatious ways. Obviously, a lot had changed in the few years since we'd first gotten close. I wasn't just your average newly single eighteen-year-old girl. I had a child with my ex-boyfriend, and I hadn't even started to recover from what a rocky road that had been. I had more reasons than ever to be cautious of starting a new relationship. I also had more reasons than ever to appreciate the trust, friendship, and chemistry I had with Kyle. I didn't know where it would lead, but I had no desire to change the course.

CHAPTER 12:

IF YOU'RE FEELING

remind me how this distance works
so close yet so far
no plan but to just be us
if you listen it's perfect
but if you're feeling
it hurts

remind me how to love again
to be selfless and fearless
warm and excited
if you listen it's exciting
but if you're feeling
it's worry

remind me how to be open
wounded yet numb
willing to be known
if you listen it's terrifying
but if you're feeling
it's strength

you don't have to remind me
of how we ended up here
listening to my mind
while feeling my heart

so if you're listening i care about this
and if you're feeling i'm in love with you.

CHAPTER 13:

HOME IS WHERE YOUR MOM IS

Bentley and I moved back into my parents' house, which was bittersweet considering the reason, but comforting for the change in atmosphere. Actually, it was in my parents' house where Bentley had one of his biggest moments. I had him in the kitchen with my mom and my brother, and he was crawling around in the cutest little outfit. While we were all eating and chatting, Bentley started pulling himself up by the edge of the table and sort of walking himself around it.

I got excited right away. Bentley had only started crawling a month or two before that, when he was between eight and nine months old. It was a little later than I'd heard it was supposed to happen, and he never really got as far as moving around on his hands and knees. It was always an army crawl where he'd be on his elbows and his knees, just scooting himself around. That had me a tiny bit worried. But he was fast! It was another interesting little milestone once he figured out how to move himself around, because I got to see what he was really interested in. It was fun just seeing how he explored. And just a few weeks later, when he was around ten months old, he was trying to make his way around the table. I could tell he was getting it figured out, so I said, "Okay, we've got to try this."

My mom and brother and I went and gathered around him just a couple of feet away from each other, and we just took turns holding him up, letting him get his balance, and letting him go. At first he just stood there for a minute, wobbled, and fell over. That happened a couple of times. But then, he finally took his first step.

It was so, so sweet. Even though it was only about a centimeter of a step forward and his feet hadn't really come off the ground yet, you could see in his face how proud he was that he was doing it. We stayed there and let him practice for a little bit, and then it seemed like thirty minutes later he was running around all over the place. It must be quite a feeling to walk for the first time. No wonder toddlers go so crazy with it. That kind of independence and progress would go to anyone's head.

I was feeling like I could use a dose of that for myself. So far, I was still wobbling. After I'd had some time to decompress from the breakup and steady myself a little, I wanted to make more of an effort to get off my lonely planet. My friends and family were a big help, and without a failing relationship on my list of daily concerns, I had more time and energy to make room for some fun in my life. My girlfriends convinced me to go out and embrace being single. It didn't come naturally at first. They almost had to train me back into it. It took a lot of their persuading for me to realize I could do whatever I wanted with my free time now. Without them pushing me, I probably would have just switched back into my "I don't want a boyfriend" mode indefinitely.

But I wasn't a high school sophomore anymore. I realized I could go out with friends and talk to guys and flirt, without having to get into a relationship or get physical. Neither one of those was a top priority, so it was nice to figure out how fun it could be just to flirt and date as an adult. Of course it's nice to get that kind of attention, even if there are no real feelings involved.

Maybe especially when there are no real feelings involved. I figured out that I had what some people call a guy personality when it came to those kinds of expectations. I wasn't interested in the seriousness of it. I didn't even think actual relationships should be overly serious. Of course they required commitment and honesty, but they're also supposed to be fun. And fun was the only thing I really counted on when I was out meeting new people. My priority was to have a positive mindset and put myself in positive situations. I felt literally no pressure or urgency to hunt for my next man.

Of course, there was something else that came into play. Bentley definitely changed how I looked at relationships. Even if I had been in a hurry to find someone new, it looked like a challenging prospect. It's difficult to get into relationships when you have a child. You can't just go around and date all week. You can't pick up and go to a movie at the drop of a hat. Everything has to be planned and scheduled. And I wouldn't have been able to see anyone all the time like couples usually do in the beginning, because I wasn't going to take Bentley to be around someone I didn't know well. That meant the only time I had to socialize was when Bentley was with Ryan's parents. There were just a lot of restrictions that would have made it impossible to date in a way that was normal for someone my age.

When you're eighteen or nineteen and you don't have a kid, you run around taking chances and exploring. You can be boyfriend and girlfriend without knowing how serious it is, and if it doesn't work out, you just move on. But when you're a teen mom, you can only pursue someone if you're really, really interested, and if they're serious enough to figure out how to work around the responsibilities and obligations of parenthood. You have to know you'll be in it for the long haul way sooner than you'd have to know if you didn't have a kid. That can be very, very tricky. Frankly, it didn't even seem worth the effort.

I went on a couple of dates after Kyle and I broke up. They were cool guys, but it just didn't click. When you meet someone, either the connection is there or it's not. If it's there, you'll treat each other right and want to be with each other. If it's not there, it's going to be bullshit. I've always felt like I could easily decipher the difference between serious interest and "You're cute and I'm bored, so let's meet up Saturday night." I was fine with the second one as long as it was fun, but I never counted on anything more. Especially since the more guys I met and talked to, the clearer that "connection" element became in my mind. The fact was I'd never stepped into a relationship without it. With Kyle it was based on friendship, but it was very strong. With Ryan it was based on chemistry and hormones, but that was very strong, too. I had never known what it was like to talk meaningfully to a guy or date a guy without a ridiculously strong connection. So if I was with someone and didn't feel it, I had no motivation to spend any time taking it farther.

Some of my best friends were going to school in Nashville, and one weekend I went up to visit them. Of course I called Kyle. He wasn't racing anymore, so he was living there full time. I was thrilled to spend time with him. It felt like we finally had our old connection back, and it was the first time we'd really been able to enjoy it so fully. A lot of things were the same between us, but a lot was different, too. I wasn't a fifteen-year-old girl anymore. I was an adult, and a mom. And he'd grown up, too. But being with each other brought out something we'd both been missing. After all the crazy stuff I'd been dealing with, he made me feel kind of young again.

The trip brought back the question of the gray area in full force. Things between us were better than ever, so did we want to risk screwing it up? We were still scared to take the plunge. Besides, no matter how strongly I felt about Kyle, I was still scared of jumping into a relationship. I wanted to make sure I wasn't just doing it to fill the void of Ryan being gone. So my intention was to just have fun and make the most of our friendship.

But I was single, and I could do whatever I wanted. It would be a shame to keep wasting that all the time, and I thought, "If I'm gonna kiss anyone, it's gonna be Kyle." So before I went back to Chattanooga, I did. It was our first kiss.

That March, my mom offered to watch Bentley for three or four days so I could go down to Panama City with my girlfriends for Spring Break. Some of Kyle's friends were down there, too, so I invited him to take the trip with me. That was when, just by going with the flow, we finally took the next step. Maybe it was the magic of Spring Break in the air, but that weekend, we basically acted like we were in a relationship. We definitely weren't just single friends wilding out together. We spent the entire time with each other, and we had such a good time. Once we stopped avoiding it, it was too obvious to ignore: We were totally in love.

When the trip was over and it was time to go home, Kyle had to go back to his town and I had to go back to mine. We knew we were going to miss each other and we were both set on figuring out when we'd be able to meet again. Considering the vibe, it just seemed obvious to make it official. The conversation practically happened on its own. Once we got home, we talked about what to do next. It didn't take long to get to where we both said, "Why not? If we're so good together and neither of us is interested in anyone else, why waste any more time?"

And there we went. Almost ten years after we'd met as kids at the motocross track, and three years after we'd started to flirt with a potential romance, Kyle and I were finally together.

* * *

The idea of getting into a new relationship while being a teen mom to a toddler had always been intimidating, and I wasn't sure how I was supposed to go about it. I wasn't reading any guide-books regarding that situation. Even though Kyle and I had a history and a strong relationship, I was still hesitant about Bentley and him. I knew it would be a deal breaker if Kyle couldn't be there for Bentley and be involved. I kind of eased into it. I started testing the waters before things got serious. If Bentley was doing something funny, I'd send Kyle a photo to see how he reacted. Or we'd Skype, and Bentley would be there with me while we talked. That helped me get a feel for how Kyle was taking to him. To my relief, he always seemed very confident about it. It never felt like he was faking it or his enthusiasm was forced. He really seemed to enjoy Bentley and take an interest in him, asking me how he was and what he was doing. That took a lot of pressure off and cleared the way for us to move forward.

We moved pretty fast. Not long after we got back from Spring Break, I decided to move to Nashville for a few months.

There were different reasons for that decision. Fifty percent of it was because my best friends and Kyle were there. And fifty percent was because I'd been living back with my parents, and even though I absolutely loved them and they were an unbeliev-able source of help and support, it was probably the one and only time in my life when they kind of drove me nuts. I'd lived with Ryan for a year and a half, but when I moved back home, it was almost like they forgot I'd ever been on my own. It was the first time Bentley had lived in their house, too, and it was my first taste of someone else actually being involved in my parenting process.

I didn't expect it to be so nerve-wracking. Every day my parents would check up on every detail.

"What did Bentley eat today?"

"Did he sleep?"

"When was the last time he ate?"

"Have you changed his diaper?"

"Has he had a bath?"

It was like they forgot I'd already been a mom for a year and a half. They thought I was still completely new to it. My dad was even worse than my mom with the Bentley questions. There were times when I'd be like, "Dad. My child is alive and healthy. He's not starving. It's fine." Of course, I would never talk back to my parents or refuse to do something they told me to do, because that's just not who I've ever been. I definitely wasn't going to disrespect them while I was living in their house and they were continuing to give me an insane amount of help and support. So I could never find a way to say, "You've got to stop doing this." I didn't even think they knew they were bothering me. They were just thinking about looking out for Bentley. But it was driving me crazy.

I just wanted to get away. I wanted to be on my own with Bentley where I didn't have anyone questioning me. I wanted to be an adult. And as always, there was another side to it, as well. As much as it was driving me insane to feel like others were meddling with my parenting, I also knew I was getting too used to the help. I was so accustomed to having my parents or Ryan's parents there when I needed them that I was afraid I was becoming too dependent on that privilege. It was to the point where if I wanted to go and do anything, whether it was a night out with my girlfriends or a trip to Panama City, I had no doubt that my parents or Ryan's parents would be willing to step in and help. The last thing I wanted to be was ungrateful, but it really went back to that old lesson my mom taught me. I needed to know that I could fix my own flat tires if I had to. I just wanted to be by myself with Bentley and learn how to figure things out on my own.

The last big reason I had for moving to Nashville was the sense of loneliness that just wouldn't stop nagging at me. Even though I was looking forward to living in Kyle's city and finally being able to build our relationship, at the same time, I wanted to rediscover how to be comfortable with being alone. It was a personal goal for me. I wanted to conquer those spells of sadness and isolation that had started to drift in when I found myself alone at night. It felt like a weakness to fear being alone, and since that was such a new feeling, I wanted to believe I could find a way to beat it. I wanted to rebuild my sense of independence and the strength that came with it.

It was time for me to go out into the world and find myself. I wasn't going very far on an actual map, but it was a big positive step for me. I had the idea in my mind that if I didn't have Bentley, I would have been at college. I'd never moved away, not really, and I didn't know what it was like. To me it seemed like the act of moving to another city offered all of these milestones that would push me to be a stronger person and a better adult. The more I thought about moving to Nashville, the more hopes and possibilities I started attaching to it. In a way, my dream was that if I took that road and experienced those typical moments of self-discovery, I'd fix everything up and I'd be happy.

Before I moved I had a job at a high-end restaurant in Chattanooga. Combining that with some of what I made through MTV, I was able to save up a good amount of money for Nashville. By May, I was ready to make the move. So I packed up with Bentley and off we went.

CHAPTER 14:
A BEAUTIFUL MESS

When you want to start fresh and there's a big mess in your way, it's always going to get worse before it gets better. The deeper you are in your problem and the less sure you are of how to deal with it, the more this is true. For me in Nashville, it took awhile before I started being able to see through the dust and clutter and start looking ahead with more confidence. But I was excited from the get-go to start the mission.

I moved into a house about a twenty-minute drive from Kyle's, which was a considerably more comfortable distance than the three hours that was between us when I lived in Chattanooga. And it wasn't too close, either. The point of Nashville was not to be around Kyle twenty-four seven. It was to find my bearings, on my own — with Bentley, of course — in a stable setting where there wasn't so much interference. That was my goal, and I dived right in.

Just as I hoped, putting some space between me and Chattanooga allowed me to relax and think freely about my own attitude and plans for the future. That was how Nashville helped me. It was kind of like being able to drive by myself for the first time after I'd been stuck with a learner's permit for way too long. Figuring out how to be a good mom, a grown adult, and an independent person in Chattanooga was like trying to become a better driver without ever heading out of the neighborhood. How much can you learn from turning the same corners over and over? Especially when every day brings the same traffic jams and jerk drivers, not to mention a bunch of other people in the car reminding me when to hit the breaks or turn on the blinker. Somehow I'd managed not to crash the car, but I was long overdue to hit the open road. That was what Nashville felt like. It wasn't instant perfection, but it felt good to be in a new place with Bentley where I could soul search a little bit.

Parenting brought new challenges, pleasures and surprises all the time. Bentley was just a summer and change away from turning two, which opened up our life to a little more variety. He was getting to the point where I could take him to the playground and push him on a swing and run around. There was no shortage of fun or cuteness. But again, your child can't be your best friend. At least, especially not at that age. It's not as if there's room for real conversation with a kid so small. It was always fun and rewarding to run around the park and play, and it was a happy distraction from the things that were troubling me. But at the same time, I couldn't shake the melancholy feeling that it shouldn't have been just me and him. My relationship with Kyle was not in any way a magical solution. We were off to a great start, but for the time being, there was still a void and an ache I felt when I had to remember I was still on my own in the parenting game.

It's almost impossible to be a teen mom without feeling lonely. Forget about Ryan. What about friends? None of mine had kids, so I couldn't bond with them as far as that was concerned. Our interests had split off in different directions so severely it was like a continent breaking in half. They couldn't relate to what I was going through, and I had a hard time relating to their priorities. What typical teen girl wants to talk about babies and responsibilities all the time? And what's important to them that's also important to a teen girl with a child? Growing up too fast is always lonely.

When I did meet women who had toddlers of their own, they were around my mom's age. That came with its own kind of awkwardness. I liked hanging out with people who were older than me, but I didn't want to feel like the baby of the group. Especially not in a group of moms. Women my mom's age saw me more as a daughter than a peer, and I was wary of being patronized or reminded of my age all the time. There's a reason you don't see many unmarried nineteen-year-old girls hanging out with a bunch of married couples with kids. The fact that I had one of my own didn't make the generation gap disappear. This is just one more way in which being a teen mom can be an incredibly isolating experience.

Sometimes I felt like I was missing out by not having any "mommy friends." But at the same time, moms in groups can be so judgmental. Anyone who has read the comments on any parenting article or heard about the "mommy wars" that rage online has seen as much. No matter how well you raise your kid, there will always be another parent chiming in to tell you you're on the wrong side of one issue or another. There's a fierce debate attached to just about every parenting decision, from breastfeeding to discipline to bedtimes to school lunches. It is literally impossible to avoid it. Get any group of moms together and there will almost always be some degree of side-eye in the room.

Plus, hanging out with other moms means dealing with their kids. And yes, I had my own opinions, too. Just because I keep them to myself doesn't mean I've never judged anyone else's parenting style. I've always been a no-bullshit kind of mom. I tried really hard to never let Bentley act like a moron or act up in public. I've also never been super overprotective. The way I was raised, and the way I raised him, kids were disciplined but still given the freedom to run around and learn things independently. If Bentley wanted to climb up on top of something and wouldn't listen to me when I told him it was a bad idea, I'd let him figure that out for himself. As long as I didn't see any real danger or risk of injury, it seemed more sensible to let him fall and learn from the mistake. That's just my approach. It's pointless to try and raise a kid in a bubble, and I feel it would just make it more difficult to learn his way around the world by using his own head. On the other end of the spectrum, there are plenty of moms who force people to use hand sanitizer before letting them near their kids. That's just not my thing.

Of course, I never had the option of shielding myself from all parental criticism. Not that anyone should be completely shielded from criticism. But I was on TV, and you sure as hell can't hide there.

* * *

After *16 & Pregnant* ended, I was asked to continue filming for the spinoff series *Teen Mom*. It was a tough decision. Obviously, being on MTV completely changed my life. No one expected *16 & Pregnant* to be as big as it was. No one expected a one-off documentary on teen pregnancy to turn into what it did. I didn't realize, and I'm sure the other girls didn't either, that the show would be the start of several years of pretty intense media coverage. A few talk shows are one thing. But crazy headlines in tabloid magazines? Paparazzi showing up in our towns? Thousands and thousands of viewers weighing in on our lives through social media and comments sections? None of that ever entered my mind as a possibility. But that was what happened.

As an introverted person, I wasn't happy to realize that all of these people suddenly thought of me as Maci from MTV. It felt like losing control of my ability to make my own impression on people. After I became such a public figure, I had to come to terms with the fact that almost everyone I met had already formed their own opinions of me. More specifically, a lot of them felt like they knew me. That's a double-edged sword if ever there was one. On one hand, the entire reason I embraced my place on *Teen Mom* was because I wanted to connect with others who were in my shoes, and more importantly to connect with young girls who could avoid being in my shoes. And the entire point of being the subject of a documentary is to give people a chance to know you and understand you. On the other hand, it was hard to navigate a lot of the interactions I had with people who had certain expectations of me based on what they'd seen, when for me the reality was obviously much more complex than a well-edited TV series could ever show.

It was humbling and awkward at the same time to realize that I had fans. When people approached me to introduce themselves or ask for photos, I never knew how to react. I felt like if I was super bubbly and happy to be approached, it would come off as a kind of snobbiness or a silly attitude about my own status. But I didn't want to seem unfriendly or unappreciative, either. It was hard to be graceful and humble. Then there was the fact that sometimes I was just trying to get through my day like a normal person. When you're in the supermarket with a one-year-old and you're exhausted and trying to finish shopping so you can get home and wrap up your day, it's hard to deal with strangers approaching you to talk about your life and your relationships. But I always tried to be as nice as I could. I'd be an idiot not to know that if it wasn't for those fans, I would never have had the opportunity to do the show or the platform to share my experience as a teen mom.

Plus, the positive responses have always meant the world to me. One of the biggest things that kept me going with the show was when moms in their thirties and forties would come up to me to say, "I have a thirteen-year-old kid and if it wasn't for your show coming on every week, I would never have had such a good chance to talk to them about birth control." I often heard that the show made it easier to talk to their kids about sex, pregnancy, and protection without it being as awkward as it often can be.

Then there was the other side. There were other times when I met people who said things like, "I wish that show would have been around when I got pregnant," or "If I'd known I could have been on it!" They weren't saying they wanted to get pregnant to get on TV, but they had a distorted idea of what it really entailed. Sometimes I just wanted to grab them by the shoulders and shake them. I wanted to tell them, yes, financially it was obviously a blessing, but if you've never filmed a TV show like that, you have no idea how stressful it can be. No one knows how much work it is and how exhausting it gets. It's your real life and your real struggles out there for the world to see, and the world isn't shy about commenting. How do you feel when people talk about you behind your back? How would you feel if you saw someone criticizing you in writing for everyone to see? Imagine if it was the entire world. Because that is what it feels like. When you get three million viewers a week, that many people are judging you. Someone has something to say about every little thing you do, and they don't hesitate to say it. I've read and heard it all.

The idea that the shows glamorized teen pregnancy is something I've heard countless times. It was always astonishing to me that anyone could watch the show and not see how brutal and sad it was. Many of the struggles depicted on the show were heart-wrenching. Fortunately, most people do seem to get that. The ones who watch the shows and come away thinking, "Wow, I really want to be a teen mom now," are an extreme minority compared to the rest. There was never anything on that show that could have been interpreted by any reasonable person as an advertisement in favor of teen pregnancy.

The show had an impact on my personal life, too. It definitely influenced my relationships, especially with Ryan. The dads who appeared on the show got a lot of attention, too, and it was the kind of attention that made it seem a lot more fun to be absent as a boyfriend and a dad. Then there's the fact that when you watch the show after filming, you see conversations happen that you weren't there for. It's sort of like getting to see what people are saying behind your back. That definitely created a wedge that was difficult to look beyond, and not just with Ryan. We all made an effort not to let it affect us, but it did. With a documentary series, the producers and crew get to pack up and go back home to their lives when work is done. But reality continues when the cameras are gone. The people being featured have to deal with the consequences of what's been filmed, what's been said, and what's been started. It's very difficult to keep all that in check.

Even the process of making friends changed after I started appearing on the show. Going out and meeting people, I had to learn the difference between people who wanted to get to know me as a person and people who wanted to be friends with "Maci from *Teen Mom*." Believe it or not, there are plenty of the second kind out there. But I got used to it pretty quickly, and eventually I could tell right off the bat who was who.

That was one more way Nashville made it easier for me to stretch my limbs and kind of smooth out my steering. In Nashville I had a good circle of friends I already trusted for understanding and support, including my best friend, Kyle.

Little by little, I started to straighten things out. But, again, the loneliness got worse before it got better. In fact, at first I felt more alone than ever. The main part was still the nights when I was alone and Bentley had gone to sleep. I'd sit up at nine or ten all alone and start feeling sorry for myself. But I didn't run from it. I tried to remind myself how many women out there would love to be a mom, even a single mom, and especially with a kid like Bentley. He always inspired me to fight for positivity, too. I never let myself get emotional in front of him. I couldn't be a miserable mom. I wouldn't. I was always telling myself, "You have to make it through this and be happy, because Bentley needs you to be."

What helped the most was being self-aware. Eventually I got to a point where when I started feeling lonely, I recognized it as a mood I was in and didn't let it take over my mind. It still sucked, but instead of feeling so deeply sad, I learned not to let it get me down. I wasn't a victim to it anymore. I finally started to feel like I could handle it.

CHAPTER 15:

12 THINGS YOU LEARN AS A REALITY TV STAR

1. You stop caring what you look like on camera.

In an everyday situation, I consider myself to be low-maintenance. But when I knew I was going to be on TV, of course I tried a little harder. The first few times we filmed for *16 & Pregnant*, I was putting on makeup, doing my hair, and laying out my outfits the night before. That unraveled quickly. When you're filming a documentary or reality TV and the point is to forget the cameras aren't there, you stop going out of your way to be ready for a close-up. By the third or fourth time we filmed, I was back to my usual no-makeup state. I probably didn't even brush my hair. After that, whether the cameras were on or not, I was probably in jeans and a tee shirt.

2. Your show makes all your first impressions for you.

As they say, you never get a second chance to make a first impression. It's a little nerve-wracking to think about that after you've put your life and your personality on display for millions of people. Every time you meet someone who's seen you on TV, you know they've already formed at least some trace of an opinion by the time they see you in person. It's hard to feel like you can make that important first impression when you meet someone new, because it feels like you've already made it on half the world. And there are no take-backs.

3. You never get used to being approached by strangers.

It's so wonderful to have fans and to meet people who say nice things about your show and what it meant to them. But even the coolest interactions with fans can make you nervous and self-conscious about how you're supposed to act. If you act bubbly and friendly like it's the most natural thing in the world, it might come across like you've started to think of yourself as a celebrity. But if you look too startled or even too laid back, you could seem cold or unfriendly. Figuring out how to be gracious and humble in those situations is actually kind of difficult.

4. You find out what people really think of you.

Have you ever wondered what it would be like to know what everyone really thinks about you? Would you want to know? When you live your life on camera for several years, you don't have a choice. I don't read articles or Google myself, but I'm still very aware of what's going on and the general public opinion. Every second I'm on camera sparks an opinion somewhere, and thanks to magazines, blogs and social media, those opinions reach my ears. Any piece of you that ends up on camera is going to spark a roar of feedback from people, and since to them you're just someone on TV, they don't hold back.

5. Your life looks different from the outside.

When I first watched *16 & Pregnant*, by the end of the episode my jaw was practically on the floor. I couldn't believe it. When we first started filming, I was innocent, pure, naive, sixteen-year-old, pregnant me. At the beginning of the episode, I thought, "I was such a child!" But by the end of the episode, I looked like a completely different person. I could actually see drastically how the experience changed me and pushed me into an early adulthood. My face, my expressions, my demeanor, the way I talked, and everything in general were noticeably different between the beginning and end of the episode, even though we'd only filmed for eight months. I already knew being a mom had changed me a lot, but I had no idea it was so obvious to everyone watching. Cameras let you see things you don't normally see. Another example was seeing how many tics and mannerisms I have in common with my mom. Also, it turns out I'm a lot more Southern than I realized.

6. People stop censoring themselves with you.

In a normal life, it would be shocking for a total stranger to run up to you, give you a hug, and start asking personal questions. Once your life has been on TV for a while, you learn to expect it. But it can be unpleasant when people lose perspective and say things they wouldn't say to anyone else. It's not ill-intentioned. But when someone I've just met asks, "So, how are things with you and Ryan?" I think, I don't know you! Even worse is when they come right out and trash Ryan. My hackles go up. I can talk about Ryan all I want, but I'm not going to hear it from a stranger. I might not like him ninety-nine percent of the time, but he's still Bentley's dad, and I still have his back in a way. The worst is when Bentley is right there beside me and some stranger comes up and casually calls his dad an asshole. It's hard to deal with people constantly forgetting that you're a real person and have a human reaction to what they say. At least they're nicer sometimes: "Oh my God, you're so much prettier in person!" Thanks?

7. You have to work harder for respect.

When the other Teen Moms and I started interacting with the media on talk shows and the like, it was sometimes really obvious that we were not being taken seriously. The hosts and interviewers always seemed to be talking down to us. We had almost everything going against us: We were teenagers, we were girls, we were pregnant teenage girls, and we were known for being on reality TV. There were plenty of people in media and entertainment who automatically thought of us as beneath them. It was hard to handle. Very quickly, my goal became to make it clear that there was no reason to treat me that way. I became very conscious of my tone, my language, the topics I spoke on, and how I presented myself so that interviewers would know I'm not about letting them talk to me without a certain level of respect. It's challenging to do that while still staying real and relatable to your audience, but it's better than being talked down to and forced to play along with someone else's condescending view of you. You can tell when media personalities are frustrated by it. Sometimes when they can't get what they want, they just shut down and half-ass the rest of the time allotted because you pissed them off by not letting them portray you the way they wanted.

8. You'll never be able to show who you really are.

The reality TV format is all about capturing the moment. It's all about what's going to happen, what's happening, and what just happened. Your thought process is never shown in any sort of depth. For instance, if they're filming you and your kitchen sink breaks, they'll show that the sink breaks, but not that you know how to fix the pipe. The next scene won't be you fixing the sink, it will be you telling someone that the sink broke and it sucked. The camera shows you reacting to problems, but not fixing them. It's very hard to show signs of intelligence in a reality TV format.

9. You have a special bond with your co-stars.

Whatever happens between us, the original Teen Moms and I share a unique connection. Only the four of us know what it's like to be in this situation and deal with what we're dealing with. The three of them are the only people in the whole world who know exactly what it's like from my point of view. No matter what kind of friction there's been between us, I don't appreciate it when people say negative things about them or expect me to do the same. I know how difficult it is to be scrutinized by millions of people, and I know some of my cast members have had it a lot worse than me. Whenever I hear someone I don't know judging one of them, I just want to say, "If I had to deal with assholes like you, I'd probably be like that, too. You're part of the problem, not the solution."

10. You get the fame, but not the fortune.

Reality TV can make you very famous, but you basically get the shit end of the deal: Everyone knows your name and talks about you, but there's no red-carpet prestige or glamorous piles of money. Once you become a so-called reality TV star, people immediately think you're a high-end celebrity and you travel the world and have a mansion and so much money and all these other things they associate with having your face on television. They think it's impossible to be a normal human being once you get a million followers on Twitter. The fact is, my real life isn't that much different from what it would have been without MTV. I still live in Chattanooga and go to Wal-Mart and buy bread and milk.

11. It affects your friends and family, too.

The media attention was confusing for the people around me at times. For awhile, every time there was a magazine headline like

"Maci Bookout Elopes in Vegas," my grandparents would call my parents. "We know these stories aren't true. But please confirm anyway." I knew I could deal with the negative parts of being in the public eye, and the judgment for being a teen mom, and all the criticism that came with being on TV. But then I became aware of the fact that my family and friends were being approached and asked the same kinds of unfiltered questions people were asking me. And of course they feel obligated to defend me when it was negative. It made me feel guilty that they were being put in certain positions that nobody wants to be in. I definitely wasn't the only one to be put on the spot.

12. You never feel like a celebrity.

I'll never forget going to the MTV upfronts. If you don't know, upfronts are the big events where television networks announce their new lineups for the next season. The first time I went, I was surrounded by entertainment people and celebrities from normal reality stars like myself to actual stars and performers. Everyone from the cast of *Jersey Shore* to Bruno Mars and Justin Bieber. I like to go into any situation as confident as I can be, but I felt like a fish out of water in celebrity situations. I didn't want to look insecure or make myself look silly, so I had to act like I belonged there and deserved to be there. But at the same time I didn't want to come across like I actually did think I belonged there and deserved to be there. It was like trying to find the right size pants to put on. It was difficult not to freak out in a room with people who are extremely famous when I'm just on a little show called *Teen Mom*. But all I could do was try to be normal Maci, and that's pretty much what I stuck with for good.

CHAPTER 16:

SETTLING FOR STABILITY

After five months of soul searching in Nashville, it was time to go home to Chattanooga. Originally I only meant to stay for the summer. I'd started taking college classes again, so the plan was to go back to Chattanooga in August when school started. But when summer came to a close, I just wasn't ready yet. I felt like I had a little more to accomplish. So I signed up to take all of my classes on Mondays and Tuesdays, so I could drive home with Bentley and he could stay with Ryan's parents for a couple of days while I stayed with my parents and went to school. But that got to be a hassle after a few weeks, and the gas costs were getting to be unreasonable. So around October, right as Bentley was turning two, I found a condo in Chattanooga and headed back home. And I brought Kyle with me.

I was never the type of girl to dream about my wedding day. Actually, the thought of planning a wedding has always seemed like the most stressful thing to me. I never had a vision of it, I guess. Although I knew I wanted to be married one day, it was never a number one priority type of thing. Of course at that point I'd already been engaged. Back when Ryan and I found out we were pregnant, we'd both felt a lot of pressure to get married. He proposed to me on my seventeenth birthday, just before Bentley was born, and my mom and I did make a few moves toward planning a wedding. But it never felt like a natural thing to do. I loved Ryan at the time and wanted us to be a family, but the engagement always felt vaguely forced. It had seemed like the right step to take, until it very obviously wasn't.

When I got together with Kyle, I never had any thoughts along the lines of "Okay, I'm entering this relationship because I'm gonna marry him." It wasn't a top goal and the concept didn't play a big part in us being a couple. But once he moved down to Chattanooga with me and we'd been there for awhile, it started to seem like a natural thing to think about. I was very content with Kyle. We had such a long history, and the way it had unfolded meant a lot to me. We had been so close to each other when I veered off, got pregnant, and got engaged to Ryan. And then, after such an extreme interruption, we'd gotten back together. It felt like since we'd made it through all of that, we were probably meant to be together. I also had a dream of putting a family together before Bentley was old enough to realize that he didn't have a set of married parents. And if I thought of it that way, I couldn't help but hear a clock ticking.

At the time, I felt Kyle wanted to marry me, too. He was an old-fashioned type, and he seemed to have the same understanding that we were meant to be together. But as time went on, it became obvious that he had very serious commitment issues as far as marriage was concerned. Not everyone grew up with the kind of relationship model that I had with my parents. His had split up when he and his brother were teenagers. I can't speak to what kind of relationship they had, but it didn't seem to have made a good impression on him. Like a lot of people in those shoes, he was scared. Maybe he was afraid that he was going to turn out like his parents did, or that he wasn't capable of succeeding as a parent or husband. Everyone has their own kind of baggage when it comes to that stuff.

As time went on, I clearly became more ready and willing whereas he definitely did not. I'm not the pushy type, so I didn't say much on the subject. I thought the longer we were together, the more he'd realize that was the next step. We had a solid relationship, and our life seemed settled. He was always absolutely wonderful with Bentley, and was a great father figure for him. It seemed possible that once we'd continued to make it work for a while and he came to accept that he was already a good partner and a good dad, he'd gain more confidence and stop being so afraid of fulfilling his fears by ending up in an unhappy marriage. And so the waiting game began.

Meanwhile, my life had started to feel like it was on track. I was moving ahead in school, and started to dabble in subjects that I thought I might actually enjoy turning into a career. Along with my business classes, I started taking creative writing. The writing classes were a joy, but I didn't see myself making a real living writing stories, so I started looking into the journalism side of writing. Being a writer or a journalist was the second thing I imagined for myself after I'd wanted to be a chef. But after moving from creative writing to news and non-fiction, I realized it wasn't for me. Writing had always been a pleasure for me, and I hated feeling like I was forcing it. I only wanted to write what I wanted to write, and at my own pace. I knew it would be a completely different activity if I was always on deadline. And writing for anyone but myself is hard! This book is a perfect example. When I write, I want it to be as authentic as it can be and as close as possible to what I'm really thinking and feeling. But feelings can be hard to put into words, even when they're your own. Especially when they're your own. And no matter what I was writing, I've always been so picky about word choice and things like that that it could easily turn into a big ordeal. In the end, it was obvious that was not the career for me.

Finally I shifted to media technology and found my place. After being on MTV and doing the many media appearances and public speaking engagements that came along with it, I realized I could pursue what I liked about writing in other ways by communicating on camera, on the radio or in social media. Radio, in particular, became very interesting. Having been on screen for so long, I had a little camera fatigue. Like, "Why would I want to keep my face on TV?" Radio also interested me because it involves the challenge of having to entertain and hold attention without anyone seeing your expression or your gestures.

My first radio show was for an internship at a local station. It was a weekly program called *Ask Maci*. People would call in and ask questions about any and everything from parenting, being a young adult, or what Justin Bieber was doing that week. I really enjoyed it. When it was over, I found another weekly talk radio show called *Live and Local* led by a local radio host named Brian Joyce. He covers everything from politics to entertainment, and we started a segment called "Defend Your Generation." In the segment he brings up things like pop music, smart phones, and all of the dumb shit my generation gets a reputation for. When I started appearing on the show, I wasn't very good at defending anything. We always laughed about the fact that I wasn't really sticking up for my own. But most of the stuff people found ridiculous, I found ridiculous, too. Sorry!

At home, Bentley was a typical toddler. I loved watching his little personality coming out. His first obsession was Thomas the Train. I swear I watched every one of those episodes and movies about ten times. When he could barely even talk, he learned the theme song by heart and he could name every single train just by looking at their faces. I thought that was crazy, because there were so many of them! He was always into dirt bikes and monster truck toys, even back when he was supposed to be playing with the baby toys like simple blocks or big plastic fake keychains. He was making engine noises before he could make words.

We almost skipped the Terrible Twos. Except for that pacifier. It was his biggest obsession by far. The few times I tried to take it away, he freaked out so bad I thought I'd lose my mind. Over time I tried to wean him off of it, but it was a little bit difficult, because every time he went over to Ryan's house it was back to square one. It got to the point where I brought it up with a pediatrician. She told me not to worry about it and to wait until he was old enough to reason with.

Pacifiers are a blessing and a curse in that way. That paci saved my sanity plenty of times before it made me lose my mind. When he was three years old, we finally got him to let it go. Kyle's older brother was expecting a baby, a little boy, and so Kyle and I told Bentley he had to give all his pacifiers to the new baby because he really needed them. Bentley was not happy about that at all, but he managed to step up and do the noble thing.

Age three was worse than two by far. That was when Bentley finally got into his first kind of rebellious stage. His personality was coming out and he was learning what he liked and what he wanted. And, of course, he learned I wasn't the only one who could use the word "no." Once he figured it out for himself, he said it all the time. Bentley just wanted to do what he wanted, when he wanted. So, that was fun.

That period was a challenge for Kyle, too. For both of us. Sharing parenting duties is tricky. Kyle was amazing with Bentley, but when it came time for discipline, he tended to take a quiet step back. In every other way he was a natural as a father figure, but in that regard, he never felt it was his place. That bothered me. Ninety percent of the time, he was involved in Bentley's life, and when he was around Bentley he completely took on the responsibilities of acting as a dad. To me, that meant he had earned the right to make Bentley behave and treat him with respect. It was important to me to have that enforced, and I didn't like having to handle all the discipline on my own. When I was growing up, my mom would definitely keep us in check and make us behave, but she was the more lenient parent. When I was younger, I might talk back to my mom but I would never talk back to my dad. But it was a kind of balance they had. It was kind of like my mom was the diplomat and my dad was the hardass. So it was difficult for me to fill both roles, and it was especially difficult because I didn't expect to take the hardass role at all!

* * *

When we first got together, Kyle had stopped racing and he was working for a company in Nashville. He quit that job to move to Chattanooga. The plan was originally that when he moved down, I'd take care of money and bills and stuff while he found another job. But that didn't go as planned. We didn't talk about it much, because I didn't want to make him feel any more insecure than any guy already is in that situation. The last thing I wanted to do was make him feel bad about it. It didn't make sense to complain, anyway, when he was always taking care of Bentley while I was at school. It wasn't like he wasn't doing anything.

But at the same time, my own life had finally gained some focus and momentum. I was in school, the show was in full force, and I was finding tons of opportunities to pursue in the field I was studying. But Kyle didn't seem to have an ambition to do anything.

It started to feel like we were drifting into different places, and it made me uneasy.

Other red flags sprouted up here and there. Sometimes when Bentley was at Ryan's house, Kyle and I would go out with friends. And once in awhile, drama would come up at the bar or among the people around us and I would want to remove myself from the situation. But it felt like if I got uncomfortable with something, whether it was people fighting around us or me and him arguing, he didn't take me seriously. It made me feel like if shit were to really hit the fan, I couldn't be sure he would have my back. In those situations, it was like he wasn't my partner. I felt like even if he was wrong and being stupid and ridiculous, I would have his back and go home with him. I could tell him he was a dumbass in the morning, if I wanted. Whenever any unpleasantness came up, he preferred to pretend it hadn't. I didn't like how easy it was for him to tune out how I was feeling.

Considering all the time we'd spent talking since we first met, I didn't expect communication to be one of our weak spots. But any time there was an issue or an argument, Kyle would completely, one hundred percent shut down. He didn't want to talk about it, didn't want to discuss it. He wanted to push it under the rug and pretend it never happened. I really struggled with that. I didn't hold grudges when I was unhappy, but I liked to get my point across and felt I was being heard. And in the same way, I wanted him to let me know if I was doing something that made him unhappy, because I wanted to be the best that I could be in our relationship. But it was impossible for us to grow when we were absolutely incapable of talking about any problems.

Kyle just hated conflict, and he was an expert at avoiding it. But that's the kind of problem that can last a long time. It bothered me, but no matter what, we'd wake up in the morning and be fine.

In fact, we bought a house. It was an old foreclosed house that needed a ton of updating, and we got it so we could fix it up and sell it. We were still attached to each other, and our relationship was basically as strong and peaceful as ever. But once we moved into that house, the challenges started to grow. I had a lot going on, but I didn't have a regular nine to five job. In between speaking engagements, the radio show, and school, I could be at home. And since he didn't have a job, he was always there, too. That meant we were spending a lot of time together, which is often a challenge in itself. But my uneasiness with his lack of ambition made it all the more difficult. The more time we were together at home, the more I started to feel like there was a space growing between us.

We'd always talked to each other about anything and everything. We'd shared that close connection for years. But suddenly we realized it wasn't there anymore. Once our issues and struggles became about each other, we were never able to talk like that again.

CHAPTER 17:

BETTER
THAN HERE

i know i've never been good with words
except when i'm speaking on paper
so i'll allow the sound to flow
from my pen through ink like vapor

first i want to thank you
for bringing me back to my comfort zone
above my notebook, pen in hand
writing my thoughts, being alone

i'm just sorry it's under these circumstances
but know what i'm writing is to cure
and no matter how long we are apart
our love will remain pure

i hope you know what i think of you
and the person that you are
i'd like to see you grow and learn
with me only watching from afar

i'll get into what i've been wanting to say
and while you read what i'm speaking
remember no matter how much i love you
this isn't the pain that you're seeing

i'm not sure where you went
or why i let you go
i got tired of fighting for hurt
and i thought i'd let you know

maybe i'm the one who's running
not running from what we had
but to where i need to be
a place without the bad

i've missed you as my friend
thats all i want you to be
and maybe by placing you back there
i can learn to be free

crazy because i'm fine
but that is all i've ever been
i want something to feel
the satisfaction of a win

please know i care about you
but i'm so lost on what you mean
i could never turn my back on you
i just need to be alone to dream

so while i'm out there facing the world
i want you to do the same
find out who you really are
so we don't have to play this game

find yourself and i'll find me
even if it takes forever
because two lost hearts
will never make it together

and after we have lived life
as two separate souls
after we're determined as individuals
and conquered our separate goals

then maybe, just maybe
our paths will again cross
i hope that if they never do
you'll be thankful for this loss

because my wish for us is to better apart
and even if it takes us years
even if we never join again
we will both be somewhere better than here

CHAPTER 18:

FOOL ME TWICE

There are a lot of different ways to be unhappy in a relationship, and it's not always abject misery. Kyle and I had been living in the house for about four months when it became clear that we were slowly, peacefully sliding downhill. I'd been through the decline of a relationship before, but this was a completely different scenario. And while I wasn't a completely different person, I was definitely getting older and strong enough not to ignore the writing on the wall. It wasn't that we were arguing or unhappy with each other all the time. Not at all. It was just that there were issues between us that kept the relationship from being everything that a healthy relationship needs to be.

At that point, Bentley was getting older and I was getting older, too. I didn't want to waste time again trying to build or rescue a family situation when all the signs were hinting that it could be a doomed cause. It came to the stage where I knew I had to open my eyes, assess the situation, and figure out what I could do to improve it. But the choices weren't easy to dissect into pros and cons. We weren't happy, but we were content. I was unsatisfied, and I was pretty sure he was, too, but it would have been easy, technically, to stay in that relationship forever. Since he hated conflict so much, we wouldn't be arguing or fighting like Ryan and I had. But it could easily turn into a life where I gave up on trying to address problems or express my concerns, because I'd learned he would just shut down. Did I want to spend the rest of my life like that, swallowing any friction or negative feelings between us because I'd learned he refused to deal with them? I definitely did not.

But there was a lot of good going on, too, and a lot of history between us. The waters were calm, and besides, I believed that he wanted to stay together, whether he was feeling the same dissatisfaction I felt or not. It didn't matter that he was still terrified of marriage. A lot of men are like that: Commitment-phobic while still terrified of being alone. I thought he saw the writing on the wall as clearly as I did, but he wasn't going anywhere, and he didn't expect me to, either.

It didn't end the way I expected.

One night I came home very late after a trip from a speaking engagement somewhere. When I got home, Kyle and Bentley were asleep, and I got on my computer to check my email and things. Kyle's Facebook was on the screen. I have never, ever in my life been the type of person to go through someone's phone or stalk their social media accounts. In my mind, if you have to do something like that, then why even be with that person? But when I looked at the screen, the pop-up chat windows were right there on the screen. Kyle had been talking to a girl he'd been with before he and I were together. And the talk was not appropriate. At all.

"You've got to be kidding me," I thought. "This is a joke." But the words felt flat in my head. I wasn't even sure if I was shocked, or mad, or upset. I literally just closed the computer, and I knew I was going to be gone.

Instead of making a fuss or giving him the chance to talk me out of it, I just took Bentley and went to my parents' house. When he woke up, we'd gone. I spent that night looking up houses for rent. It was surprisingly unemotional. It sucked, but I didn't cry and I wasn't mad. It just seemed like a sign. I thought, "This is what you needed. Go ahead and leave."

This was the crazy thing: Kyle never said a word about it. Not about the girl. Not about me leaving. I don't know what he thought. Maybe he realized what I'd seen, somehow, or maybe he thought I'd seen even more than I did. Maybe he got on Facebook and figured out his chats had been seen. Maybe the girl saw his account online when I turned it on, and asked him about it, and he pieced it together. Or maybe he'd just already prepared himself for the possibility of me finding out what he was up to. But when I went back to the house and I was getting some of my stuff, he didn't even ask me what I was doing. He just stayed in the bedroom, hanging out. We didn't say a word to each other until I went to the door right before I left.

"Just so you know," I said, "me and Bentley are moving out. I'll get the rest of my stuff out as soon as I can."

Kyle said, "Okay."

That was it.

That was not a normal way to break up under any circumstances, but especially not ours. After all the time we'd known each other, it was completely bizarre for the relationship to end in one matter-of-fact sentence and an "Okay." If I had needed proof that our communication problems were serious, there it was. Kyle obviously didn't want the confrontation, and I didn't see any point to it. I'd had enough. I was finally over it. I was tired of being unsatisfied. I had wanted to be with him, even wanted to marry him. But I knew when to recognize that things weren't going to change. The longer we stayed together, the further away we got from each other. My ambivalence was part of my own problem. Who knows how long I would have stayed if he hadn't messed up and given me a solid reason to leave?

My parents were shocked by the breakup. Almost everyone was. One day everything was normal, and a few days later I was all different. After a couple of overnights at my parents' house, I called my mom and said, "Just FYI, Bentley and I have moved out. This is how it's gonna be."

"What the hell are you talking about?" She didn't know where to start. But at that point I'd already made so many moves that there was nothing anybody could say or do to try to change my mind. They were confused, but they accepted it and moved on.

Then, some people were less surprised than others. Once again, when the relationship was over, I started to hear all those things I didn't need to hear. That girl wasn't the only one he'd been talking to. But it was fine. I was done. It was over. And I knew that was for the best.

I had no idea how long I would have tolerated that miserable contentment if he hadn't given me an excuse to leave. All I was looking for was a reason to go. For all our issues, it just hadn't felt bad enough to take that step. I needed a legitimate, clearcut reason to back up my gut feeling, and thankfully I got it. If I hadn't seen that Facebook chat, God only knows how long we would have lasted before something came up.

Those kinds of relationships are everywhere, and most of the time, I think people stay in them. I could understand why. I think it comes from being afraid that if you leave, you'll be thinking, "Was it really bad enough to leave? What if it actually doesn't get better than that? What if? Why did I do that?" It's hard enough even when you do have a reason, but at least a reason helps to anchor your decision. Without it, you just have to make a leap of faith in your own judgment, and that can be an extremely difficult thing to do.

But the more comfortable you are in your independence, the easier it is. That was exactly the reason why I'd worked so hard to reclaim my strength and my confidence in being alone. I wasn't afraid to be single. I wasn't afraid of losing Kyle if the evidence showed that was the right thing to happen. Ultimately, I could have thanked him for making it easier. His complete non-reaction to me was a big help. I didn't expect crying and begging, but I thought, "He's not even going to try to talk to me, or even attempt to figure out what's going on?" That made it clear that if he ever did give a worthwhile damn about us, he wasn't going to show it. So that was that.

Anyway, I always hated living in that house. I was glad to get out, even though I was pissed off by the mess it became when we broke up. Since he was older and had more credit, it was bought in his name, but I paid for it and invested a lot of money in fixing it up. For a year or two after he moved back to Nashville, he still owned the house but rented it out. That was the last thing I heard.

Marriage is definitely good for some things, like making financial decisions and buying property together. I lived and learned that lesson the hard way.

* * *

My next move was moving into a big rental house with four bedrooms and had a couple of girlfriends move in. It was laid out in a way that was perfect for sharing, almost like living in a cozier indoor version of a little apartment building, except the neighbors were people I knew and liked. Bentley and I had two bedrooms and a bathroom on the second floor, and the girls were paying me rent. It was a good foundation for a fresh start.

I was so ready to be by myself. I wanted to keep working on figuring out what I wanted to do. School was in full swing and a career would be next, and in the meantime, I wasn't interested in being someone's girlfriend again. I was just trying to focus on Bentley and myself. And since he was going over to Ryan's parents' house every other weekend, I finally found myself with a little space to have fun as an actual grown-up, going out and doing my thing without having to worry about a partner. I wasn't a hundred percent sure of what direction my life was going in, exactly, but it was kind of nice to be able to figure things out as I went.

And then, of course, there was Ryan.

Ryan was pretty excited when he heard Kyle and I broke up. Not because he was jealous and wanted to be with me, but because he and Kyle never liked each other. It was a "good riddance" for him, despite the fact that he was never around me often enough to have a real reason to dislike anybody I was with. But he had his own relationship issues going on. At that time he was dating a girl who was not at all comfortable with my existence. Ryan and I communicated at an absolute bare minimum, and only ever about Bentley. But she wasn't about that at all. If I could manage to get him to pick up the phone when I called about something, she'd wind up mad at him and then he would act like it was my fault.

The thing about having a kid with someone as a teen is that your relationship with that person becomes a permanent part of your life whether you like it or not. Even if you were in a situation where you never saw him again, the connection of sharing a child carves him into your brain for good. Ryan and I would always have something to do with each other's lives whether we wanted it that way or not. That didn't stop him from putting as much distance between us as possible. It didn't matter that the only time I ever reached out to him was when I was asking him to pick Bentley up from somewhere or spend some time with him. It didn't matter what Bentley needed or how important it was. I could never count on him to answer the phone or return a text, much less show up. A lot of the time, the only communication Ryan and I had was on camera. There were long periods of time when if we hadn't been filming a show together, he would never have spoken to me at all.

That would have been okay with me, if not for the fact that he wasn't always present for Bentley, either. Even though Bentley went to Ryan's house on the weekends, it was always clear that he was really going to visit Ryan's parents, Jen and Larry. Because if being a dad was anything less than a hundred percent fun, easy and convenient, Ryan didn't seem interested. The only time he seemed to wake up and take an interest in parenting was when he felt like he had nothing better to do. As soon as something more fun came along, or something that seemed like less work, Ryan took it as an excuse not to show up.

It was inexplicable. Bentley was growing up to be such a cool kid. He was doing great in pre-school. All his teachers loved him. His personality was taking shape, and he was a lot of fun. He even got into baseball, which was a blast. Little League baseball for kids who are five and six years old is really just for parents' entertainment. It was so funny to watch the early games where the kids were just running around like little goofballs instead of playing by the rules. One kid would hit the ball and instead of running for first base, he'd chase after the ball he'd just hit instead. Or it would land in the outfield near two kids who were too busy building castles in the dirt to notice. It was hilarious.

When Bentley got a little older and started wanting to learn the game for real, that was even more fun. We spent all day one spring out in the yard practicing. He went on to make the all-star team and play all summer long. It was cool to watch him get the hang of it, and since I'd been so into softball, I was especially excited when he got obsessed with baseball.

Things really were turning out okay. Being a teen mom hadn't ruined my life. I'd managed to get through the worst of it and grow up. Now I wasn't a teen mom at all. I was just a mom. I was older and wiser, and I'd grown confident in my role. I'd settled in, and I was happy being Bentley's mom. But there was a blank space in the picture that I just couldn't ignore.

Why couldn't Ryan see what he was missing?

CHAPTER 19:

REPLAY

replaying years in mind
knowing what went wrong
remembering that night
aware we weren't that strong

letting myself go
allowing ownership to you
forgiving struggles created
still something i'd never undo

wish it had been known
the pain love could create
question always asked
would i go back and wait

shared time and experience
with what is most beautiful to me
world full of happy sacrifice
person i came to be

what is known now
i wouldn't go back and wait
i'd take the same result
only with someone i don't hate

CHAPTER 20:

COPING WITH CO-PARENTING

Being a single mom isn't the end of the world. Not for the mom, and not for the kid. Countless kids have grown up happy and loved with one or even both biological parents out of the picture. Single parents, grandparents, and adoptive parents wind up in the driver's seat for many different reasons. All families are different, and there's no shame in having an arrangement that doesn't fit the stereotypical ideal of two happy, healthy, responsible parents who stay together until they die of old age. There's nothing wrong with seeing the value in that, either, or in striving for it. But if it doesn't work out, it's still perfectly possible to be a good parent and raise an amazing kid.

Fine and good. That doesn't make it any easier to watch a parent flat-out refuse to parent for no discernible reason.

It wasn't something I could just get over, because it was never going to be finished. Ryan would always be Bentley's father, and as time went on, that fact would only take on more meaning. The worst part was the helpless feeling that each passing day brought Bentley closer to having his first real thoughts and feelings about Ryan's absence. It was one thing when Bentley was too young to grasp the situation or form lasting memories of his home life. But Bentley turned three, turned four, turned five, and each year brought him closer to being able to consider the situation for himself. When would that happen? I was always wondering and dreading. Would he make it through pre-school without noticing that other kids knew their dads as well as they knew their moms?

When would he pick up on it? When would he start to care? When would it start to hurt?

Was it so crazy for me to keep hoping Ryan would come back around and start parenting? How could I give up on it when there was still a chance for him and Bentley to make a connection before the damage became irreparable? And how could I come to terms with Ryan's perspective when I couldn't find a way to make sense of it? I often found myself circling back to the thoughts that had flickered in my mind back when I was just a teen: He and I had it so much easier than other people in our situation. Yes, we'd been unprepared for parenthood. Yes, it sucked to grow up before we were supposed to. But Ryan had more control and freedom to enjoy being Bentley's dad than most young dads can even dream of. That wasn't supposed to be the case, but it was. He didn't have to lift a finger if he didn't have to. Between me, my parents, and his parents, the diapers were changed and the work was done. We had a TV show providing us with income. He didn't even have to deal with me! I'm not perfect, but I'm not some crazy baby momma, and I was more than happy to leave him alone.

Everyone around him was taking care of the hard stuff. It would have been so easy for him to participate. And yet he wouldn't even take on the fun stuff, like when Bentley started playing baseball. On a Friday night went Bentley had baseball practice and plans to spend the weekend at Ryan's house, it was Ryan's mom Jen who met me at practice, and it was Jen and Larry he went home with. When Bentley had a game the next day, it was Jen and Larry at the game and Jen and Larry driving him home again. Ryan almost never even stopped by. Bentley never expected him to.

I couldn't make myself okay with the fact that my co-parent wasn't Ryan, but Ryan's parents. Yet that was the reality. Once upon a time I had hoped that when Ryan and I broke up, it would allow him and Bentley to get closer together. If I was really the reason he was so miserable in that house with us, fine. Then surely if I wasn't there to terrorize him, he'd be free to approach Bentley and their emotional relationship would finally develop a little bit. And if that wasn't enough, if the enthusiasm still wasn't there, then I hoped at least he'd have no choice but to step up at least a little bit as a father, considering that from then on all his time with Bentley would be spent without me there to take care of things by default. Essentially, I had hoped the one good thing that would come out of our breakup would be that Ryan and Bentley would finally spend some time together one on one.

Unfortunately, that didn't happen. Instead, Ryan's mom Jen picked up right where I left off. Both of Ryan's parents were instantly dedicated to Bentley and involved themselves completely in his life. I was extremely grateful for their support, but at the same time, they were supposed to be grandparents, not co-parents. Since they were so willing to take care of Bentley in Ryan's place, it was extremely easy for him to stay disconnected and uninvolved.

For a long time, I didn't feel like they were willing to stick up for me when Ryan was being Ryan. But Jen and Larry were also in an extremely difficult position. I had full custody of Bentley, and there was no court order or anything in place that guaranteed them time with their grandson. Meanwhile, Ryan was supposed to be their main link to Bentley, and yet he preferred to remain on some other faraway planet. To put it bluntly, if I had been a crazy woman, I could have taken Bentley somewhere and said, "You're not seeing him unless you get a judge to make me." There would have been nothing they could do about it, unless Ryan actually took me to court.

In the beginning they didn't know me or trust me enough to be comfortable with that situation, and who could blame them? So there was a time when instead of being upfront about Ryan's behavior, they played both sides of the fence with the intention of getting Ryan to fight for those visitation rights. They were just afraid of not having any established connection to Bentley. Who could hold that against them?

But as the years went on, they realized I would never take Bentley from them or them from Bentley. I would never make Bentley pay for the fact that Ryan got on my nerves. Once that was clear, they were more on my side. We've always been on the same side, really, even if we disagreed in places.

And we did. I wished to God Ryan's parents would make him take responsibility. I wished to God they would have handled it the way that I think my parents would have. Because unless I was a drug addict who ran off and disappeared and they didn't know if I was alive or dead, my parents would never have let that responsibility fall on them. They warned me of that the day I told them I was pregnant, and they meant it. Not because they didn't enjoy being with Bentley or enjoy helping me, but because that wasn't how they raised me. They didn't raise me to be the type of person who would dump my responsibilities on whoever was willing, just so I could run around doing whatever I wanted. It was because they wouldn't be able to stand the sight of me willfully disconnecting myself from my child.

If the roles were reversed, if Ryan had full custody of Bentley and I was the one avoiding all my responsibilities, my parents would have done whatever they could to make sure Bentley was cared for. It's just that in their world, that would include fighting tooth and nail to make me accept my role as his parent. Because that was what was best for Bentley: Both parents taking care of him. Both parents showing him they loved him. Both parents helping him grow. Both parents making it absolutely clear that he was wanted and appreciated. That was what he needed. Having two amazing sets of grandparents would never erase or cover up the fact that Bentley was going to grow up possibly thinking of his father as a guy who never seemed to want to be there. That was what broke my heart, and that was what made it hard to just be grateful for Jen and Larry's help.

We worked hard to build a healthy relationship and not let Ryan's behavior interfere, but it was hard to stay out of that shadow all the time. It caused tension in strange ways. What drove me crazy was when they'd spoil Bentley on his visits. All grandparents spoil their grandkids, but that doesn't mean letting them get away with murder. From what I saw at their house, if he wanted to act like a little shit, that was fine. If he wanted to talk back, that was fine. There was very little discipline. And of course, all I could see was them treating Bentley just like they'd treated Ryan. How on Earth could they not see the problem with that? In the years since Bentley was born, we'd all had front row seats to the heartbreaking consequences of Ryan doing whatever he wanted and never having to answer for it. And yet they saw no problem being just as indulgent with Bentley as they'd been with Ryan. I felt like I tried to get them to take a different approach. If I saw Bentley talking back to Jen or acting a certain way when I was there picking him up or dropping him off, I'd get on him, and he'd straighten up. So I'd turn to Ryan's parents and say, "Don't let him do that! Quit letting him act like that!" But it was no use, and I couldn't put it any more strongly than that. What could I say? This is how shitheads are made?

All differences aside, we did our best to develop a relationship and do right by Bentley. There was only one time when the friction over Ryan came to a head. One night I was in the kitchen at Ryan's house with him and his mom, dropping Bentley off. Ryan and I had been arguing about something, since that was all that happened when we had to talk. He said something rude to me, and his mom spoke up to say, "Okay, that's enough, you need to quit." And right there in front of her, he called me a bitch. She started to get onto him for it, and he just walked out of the house, slammed the door, and went for his truck. And she just gave up and let him go.

For whatever reason, it was the straw that broke my back. "He's like this because you let him be," I snapped. "The only reason he acts like this is because you let him get away with it. You let him talk to you like this. You never make him do anything. You never tell him to be an adult." I really went off, loud and angry, and then I stormed off, too, and left her in tears. She didn't argue with me, and we never talked about it again. But it wasn't like my feelings had ever been a secret, and it wasn't like she was blind.

Ryan's parents weren't clueless about who he was becoming. They had their own understanding of the situation. Obviously, they'd known him all his life. At the same time, Ryan was their little boy just like Bentley was mine. And at that point, I couldn't expect them to control his behavior. He was a grown man. What was Jen supposed to do? Drag him back and give him a spanking? Turn her back on him? It was too late to demand that he become a different person, when he'd had all his life to build up certain entitlements and expectations. You can't stop a grown-up from acting like an asshole if that's what he truly wants to do.

I lost plenty of sleep wondering what it would have been like if Ryan's parents hadn't stepped in after Bentley was born. Would Ryan have grown up a little, if they hadn't been there to pick up the slack for him? Or would his behavior have been the same? I hated to consider it, but I had to acknowledge the possibility that having Jen and Larry take on the co-parenting role might actually be the best-case scenario. After all, what if they hadn't stepped in and Ryan hadn't stepped up? Or what if he had done more for Bentley, but been even more resentful for it? Would it have been a nightmare situation where Bentley didn't get all that love and care when he was away from me? What if instead of a non-existent relationship, they had one that was even more emotionally damaging? I couldn't confidently guess what really would have happened if Ryan's parents hadn't been there.

I came to terms with the way that it was, at least as best I could. I had to stop taking out my frustration with Ryan on them. It wasn't worth hurting their feelings. They've always been great people, and Bentley and I have both been blessed to have them. Anyway, it wasn't their fault. Ryan wasn't their fault. No one outside of him could be blamed for his apathy toward parenting. It was foolish to blame an outside factor for his apathy. I couldn't pretend I understood it in the first place. No one could. There was no explanation for his absence from Bentley's life.

But I had to make some sense of it to keep from losing my mind. I thought about it and thought about it as time went on. For the first couple of years, when Bentley was still young and Ryan was younger himself, I chalked it up to immaturity and an undeveloped parental instinct. He didn't know what to do, and he didn't have the nurturing drive, so it was easy for him to slink back and leave me in the driver's seat full time. Then, when we split up and Ryan still wasn't motivated to step up for Bentley, I concluded he was just procrastinating. It wasn't hard to imagine him thinking, "My parents are dealing with it, and Bentley's too young to know the difference. So I'll just keep having fun for awhile until it actually matters."

As Bentley got older and Ryan still didn't make any moves toward building a stronger relationship with him, I could only guess that he felt like he'd missed his chance. Maybe Ryan imagined he'd be ready to be a dad once Bentley was walking and talking, but since he'd never bothered to practice, he couldn't figure out how. And since Bentley had already learned not to see him that way, he wasn't approaching Ryan or asking him to be anywhere. Maybe that made Ryan think, "I'm obviously not needed, so never mind." Maybe in his eyes, the ship had already sailed.

I couldn't read his mind. I didn't know what he was thinking. But one thing was for sure: Ryan's absence did affect Bentley's view of him. There was no getting around it. If Jen and Larry couldn't come to a baseball game, Bentley would ask where they were and why they didn't come. He never asked why Ryan wasn't there. Never. It was like it didn't occur to him. But that wasn't the end of it. There were times when the stars aligned and Ryan agreed to come and pick Bentley up for a weekend at his family's house. I barely noticed at first when Bentley started to ask who was coming to pick him up. When I told him it was Jen, he said, "Oh, okay." But then one day I said his daddy was picking him up, and he didn't like it. If Ryan was coming, he didn't want to go.

Just as I'd feared, time had run out. Bentley had gotten old enough to start having feelings about the situation. The fact that they were negative feelings was a hard pill to swallow.

CHAPTER 21:

DON'T JUST EXIST, *LIVE*

One weekend in September, about nine months after Kyle and I broke up, I went down to Texas with my best friend Raj to visit our friend Casaundra. We spent the weekend hanging out with her and her best friend, a guy named Taylor. I'd actually met Taylor once before, briefly, when the same four of us had happened to be in New Orleans back in spring for a Supercross race. Yes, once again, it came back around to dirt bikes.

The first thing that stood out to me about him was that he had no idea who I was. After he'd been around me for a second and saw people taking pictures of me, he figured out I was on TV. But he never so much as brought it up. He just treated me like I was Maci, some girl he'd met with his friends. It was a breath of fresh air to be around someone new, who didn't give a shit about the TV show I was on.

Down in Texas, as the weekend went on, I thought, "I kind of like this guy." We all had a really good time, and to me it was obvious he was a big part of the reason. It wasn't like hearts flew out of my eyes, but I really liked him. As far as I could tell, everybody did. It seemed like everywhere we went, everyone loved Taylor. I was impressed and kind of intrigued. I liked the way he carried himself and put everyone at ease.

Since Kyle, I hadn't talked to anyone or dated anyone that I'd been interested in. But Taylor was different. I'd never spent time with a guy who was so completely easy to be around. He was down for whatever, no demands and no complaints. I've always tried to be friends with everybody. I don't do gossip or drama, and I like to have a good time with a minimum of negativity. But people can be a pain in the ass. There's always someone dying to share their negativity with you or put the brakes on a fun night when they get mad about something. But Taylor seemed to have the same attitude as me. He was just down for the ride and wanted things to be cool.

The four of us hit it off so well that he was actually the one to drive Raj and me to the airport when we left. As we said goodbye, I knew that I wouldn't mind seeing him again. At some point during the weekend when we'd all been hanging out and running around, I'd gotten his number. Sometime after I got home, I started texting him. He texted me back, and after that the conversation never stopped.

Casaundra and Taylor made plans to come down to Chattanooga for Halloween. Once again, we all had a really good time all weekend. After almost two months of flirting over text, we got a chance to flirt in real life.

The last night before Taylor and Casaundra went home was Halloween night, and we had a big party. Taylor and Raj dressed up as nerds in high-water khaki pants, glasses, polo shirts and suspenders. Plus some weird socks. And three of my good friends and I decided to be Ninja Turtles. None of us wanted to do the skanky costume thing, but we didn't want to be full-fledged turtles, either. So we made it cute. We had tank tops in the perfect turtle green with Ninja Turtle abs spray-painted on the front, and tall green socks to match. Then we all had spandex shorts in the turtle colors. I was Leonardo, so mine were blue. I had a blue bandana tied around my forehead karate style, blue bands around my elbows and knees, and blue Converse sneakers. For the shells, we went to Wal-Mart and got some of those huge foil roasting pans, spray-painted them green, and tied them on like backpacks. And then we got our weapons. It turned out amazing.

When everyone had left or gone to sleep, Taylor and I lay down in the one bed left and talked all night. Even though we were alone in a bed and there'd been plenty of drinking, he never tried to kiss me or creep close to me or anything like that. I've never been one to get physically involved with someone outside of a relationship, but most guys will try something. I had so much respect for him that he was able to hold a conversation with me without the slightest hint of pressure to do anything but talk. You have to give credit to a guy who can resist putting the moves on a Ninja Turtle. We just had a great time with each other, and when he left the next day, I got that feeling like we'd made a connection.

Raj and I planned another trip to Texas for late November. Leading up to that, Taylor and I started to chat more about dating and relationships. By the time Raj and I went back down to visit, it was obvious we were interested in each other. We didn't say anything about it, but it was pretty plain to see. I spent every night that weekend in Taylor's room, although somehow we didn't do anything more than kiss. Once again, he was just totally laid back and made me feel like he wasn't expecting to get anything physical from me. By the end of it, I was even starting to get a little weirded out. I was like, "Why hasn't he even tried anything yet? Is he not even thinking about it? This is getting awkward." Finally I brought it up.

"I just respect you and what you wanna do," he said, "so I'm not gonna push you to do anything." After we talked for awhile, I realized that just as much as I respected him not trying anything, he respected me for the same reason. If I didn't want to give it up, he'd only respect me more.

And that was good, because as I told him: "Until we're serious or I just can't take it anymore, you're not getting anything out of me." I wasn't trying to put him to the test, but it was nice to know he could handle it. When I went back home to Chattanooga, it felt like a good cliffhanger. We were both dying for the next chapter.

The next time I went back to Texas was in December, right around Christmas time. Taylor asked me to be his girlfriend, and there we went. It was official. Before I knew it I ended up at his house when his whole family was there for dinner, so I met them all. Grandparents, aunts, uncles and cousins. I was freaking out a little bit inside, but at that point I felt like I knew him so well that I knew it was going to be okay. In fact, I already wanted to meet them. I figured if I liked him and his morals and beliefs and how he feels about life, I was more than likely going to like his parents. And I did. The crazy thing was that they reminded me of my own parents. To me that was nothing but a good sign, and we just kept going from there.

Long-distance relationships are kind of nice when they start out long-distance. All we did was talk and text all the time, and I got to know so much about him before we really even got started in person. And we got to do it without friends being involved or photos being all over social media. Nobody had input into our relationship as it started except the two of us. In a way, it was sort of an old-fashioned courtship. It was a nice way to get to know each other without all of the bullshit that can get in the way.

Our personalities and our way of interacting with each other made long-distance easier. From the beginning, it was a more mature and adult relationship than anything I'd ever experienced. There was no drama, and he was never playing games. There was no "I'm not gonna text him first today" or "I'm waiting to call back so she doesn't think I'm too eager." None of that, ever, at all. He was open and honest with me, and I knew he was taking it seriously. I never once had to doubt what his motives were, and it was really nice.

As the months went by and we only got closer and more serious, I started letting Taylor and Bentley get to know each other a little bit. I'd take Bentley down to Texas every other time I went down on business, or on school breaks we'd drive the thirteen hours and stay there for about a week. They got to spend enough time together for us all to know that they were going to get along just fine.

After a year and a half, we were over that. It was time to get serious about what we wanted to do next. But I wasn't about to move Bentley halfway across the country. So all I could say was, "Are we going to break up, or are we going to figure out how to get you out here?" We both decided that we wanted to stay together, and he was ready to take that step. For the next four or five months, our focus was on saving money, finding him a job, and figuring out the right time to take the plunge. In the meantime, we talked a lot about how he'd fit into Bentley's life, and he was definitely nervous about the prospect of growing into more of a father figure rather than just being Bentley's friend. There were a lot of deep conversations about what he was expecting and what I was expecting.

We probably went overboard trying to prepare, but it was scary. I wound up bracing myself in a way that told me I was carrying a lot more baggage from my past relationships than I even realized. I was afraid of things turning out with Taylor the way they'd been in the past. I was scared that once he moved in we'd end up miserable and start fighting all the time. Or maybe he'd realize he was a commitment-phobe after all and take off for the hills. And part of me was just afraid my life was going to be too much for him all at once. It was hard to wrap my head around him taking on such a huge change. Down in Texas, he was basically a single guy whose only responsibility was his job. Not only that, but he had an awesome life down there. Everybody knew him and liked him, and things were good. Now he was preparing to go from that to being my boyfriend, living with me and my five-year-old kid, in a new place away from his family and his friends. Frankly, I was afraid he was going to get to Chattanooga and freak out. I was waiting for shit to hit the fan.

But it never did. What I liked most about him was exactly what made it work. He's always been confident, headstrong, and a fighter, in a sense. I was glad to see that he was never interested in giving up or running away from what we'd gotten into. As for him adapting to life in a new city, the man could make friends with a wall. My parents absolutely adored him, and he loved them, too. That was one of the best things I could hope for and had never experienced. With Ryan and Kyle, it wasn't like my parents ever disliked them, but I sensed that they were mostly just supporting what I wanted. With Taylor, they liked him all on their own. Considering how much respect I always had for their opinions, that was a huge blessing.

I was still going to school when Taylor first moved to Chattanooga, and I felt like I was finally getting a handle on what I could do for a career. While I kept up with the speaking engagements around the country, I ended up moving deeper into social media. After I got so many followers though MTV, I started getting offers from companies to host social media events and things like that. There were lots of opportunities to host chats or be paid by clicks and so on. I started to work on being savvy with my postings, thinking about the best times for certain tweets and other things that could influence how people interacted with them. The work appealed to my problem-solving side. If I wanted to make a post related to babies, I could narrow in a target audience by analyzing the details: Moms in this location who have children from X age to Y age are seeing my tweets at Z time, so that's where I can get my bang for my buck. There was a surprising amount of satisfaction in solving those puzzles and seeing the results. Since I took to it so well, I started looking into the prospect of becoming a social media specialist.

While I took night classes twice a week to wrap up my media technology degree, Bentley and Taylor were home by themselves. We knew there'd be some challenges and tests involved in Bentley accepting Taylor as a parental figure. They got along fantastically well, but one night Taylor let me know there'd been a couple of times, not a lot, but a few, when he'd told Bentley to behave and Bentley had fired back with "You're not my dad."

"Oh, shit," I thought. "Here we go." We'd already discussed that it was something that would happen and that we'd have to deal with it right away. But it was something we had to work out with Bentley himself. It took Taylor having a good conversation with him along the lines of, "I'm not your dad, and I'm not trying to replace your dad. But when you say things like that, it hurts my feelings. I am here for you, and even though you might not like what I'm saying, you still have to respect me as an adult and as someone who takes care of you." Then he told Bentley that if he was ever confused or angry about anything in the world, he could talk to him about it. Taylor said to him, "You won't be wrong if you can talk about it without being disrespectful." As soon as they had that conversation, it never happened again. It was clear Bentley felt much more understanding about what was going on.

Pretty soon we weren't just acting like a family. We had become one.

The positivity and respect I found in our relationship were exactly what I'd always hoped for, but it was almost surreal to feel that standard being met after wondering for so long if I was crazy to expect so much. It turned out I hadn't been crazy at all. It was possible to find someone with warmth and integrity who wanted the same things out of life as I did and who loved spending time with my kid. And I'd done it.

After all I'd been through and all the failures I'd experienced, I finally had someone I could imagine building a life with and not fighting tooth and nail every step of the way. I could see us working together and having fun with the journey, challenges and all. Finally, at long last, I felt like I was part of a team.

And Bentley got more than a teammate. He actually got a new coach. Taylor didn't just show up to Bentley's Little League games, he dove right into heading up the team. The kids call him "Coach Taylor," but Bentley calls him "T-Money." It's hilarious. A lot of people at the games probably don't realize Taylor's not Bentley's dad, so they're probably thinking, "Why is he calling him T-Money?"

It's all good with us. When Bentley started asking what he should call Taylor "when we get married," we told him, "Taylor, Dad, T-Money, it's up to you." Bentley knows Taylor as a dad, besides the fact that he's not a biological father. Taylor's parents too, have been great as far as treating Bentley like he's their grandchild.

When I saw Taylor take on fatherhood like it was something he actually wanted to figure out and master, it was even better than anything I'd dared to hope for. I tried not to let my thoughts slide over to the same old territory, but the closer Taylor got to settling in as a co-parent, the deeper I felt that old thorn in my side. Where was Ryan? How could he stand it? Didn't it bother him to see another man filling that role in Bentley's life when he still couldn't be counted on to spend some time with the kid over the weekend? And what about later? What if years down the line Ryan did decide he wanted to show up and be a dad? Would all Taylor's work and sacrifice for Bentley go down the drain?

I started to get stressed out thinking about all of the things Ryan was entitled to as a biological father that he took for granted, that he didn't deserve. As hard and as heartbreaking as it was for me, I couldn't imagine what it was or would be like for Bentley.

But I was getting so tired of running the same old trails in my head.

In the last season of *Teen Mom*, in the very last scene of the show, I'm sitting at the kitchen table talking to my mom about Ryan and the fact that I'd spent so much time fighting something I couldn't change. And my mom says to me, "You're going to be around him for the rest of your life. You just have to let it go." That day I finally started working to accept that I couldn't fix him. I couldn't change him. It wasn't my job or my responsibility. All I could do was keep the door open, just in case he was ever ready to show up and try. I had to do the best I could on my side without letting it consume me the way it had been consuming me for almost seven years.

I tried. I really did try.

CHAPTER 22:

CHANGE OF HEART

one of those memories
i'd be smitten by reliving
i'm being followed by cupid
and he's not too forgiving

flashbacks of summertime
i've been living on those
so maybe cupid's trail
is where my heart goes

in a southern city
i've never called home
that's what you felt like
before you were gone

irresponsible actions
falling for a stranger
there was just no time
to worry about danger

i wish i knew that night
what consumed my being
warmth i'd forgotten to feel
parts of life i hadn't been seeing

fear i'd been running from
caught up to my heart
i never had a choice
from the very start

my heart i'd been neglecting
damaged, closed, and put away
but you can't help who you love
i'm still scared you're here to stay

i am in love with you
even so, i'm not dumb
you're just like the rest
so my mind will stay numb

i've never been here before
i'll never do this again
but my control was gone
before you walked in

maybe i should shut up
maybe you should stay
maybe i'm who's running
and maybe we will be okay

CHAPTER 23:

THE TIME IS NOW TO LEARN AND LIVE

Taylor and I were settled in. Marriage was almost a given, and we'd both said we wanted kids. Bentley was happy, I was happy, and we were nothing but excited when we talked about the future. It was time for me to look into something that might have an impact on what that future would look like.

Back when Bentley was about two years old and I was around twenty, I was out at a concert with my brother and a couple of friends when all of a sudden I got a terrible pain in my stomach. It was so severe and so sudden that it felt like a contraction. I thought, "What the hell is going on?" I went into the bathroom and started throwing up. It was the most painful thing I'd ever felt. It was worse than labor. I didn't even know what to do. I was practically paralyzed by it. And then it just subsided. I had no other symptoms, no fever, nothing. But when it was over, I was actually sore. The next day I told my mom what had happened and she told me to head to the walk-in clinic and tell them what was going on.

I followed her advice, as usual. The doctors took my blood and gave me an exam, and then they said nothing was wrong with me. I took their word for it and wrote it off as a fluke, and I never thought about it again until a month later, when it happened again.

I was lying in bed with Bentley when the pain hit me just like it had the first time. Only this time it lasted longer. It lasted all night long. I ended up in the emergency room, where they did an X-Ray and took my blood and all kinds of different things. But they didn't find anything, and the pain went away eventually. Once again, I was left with no answers. It was at the emergency room where a doctor suggested that I go to an OB/GYN and have an ultrasound.

I had never had a normal period in my life, ever. By that I mean I barely even had one at all. I would get my period every four to six months, if that. It had always been that way. The ultrasound told me why: I had a bunch of cysts on my ovaries. Everyone gets them, but in a healthy menstrual cycle, they dissolve without causing any trouble. But I wasn't ovulating, so the cysts were just staying on my ovaries and multiplying. When one ruptured, that was when I felt the pain.

It turned out I had polycystic ovary syndrome. To treat it, they put me on Depo Provera birth control injections, which helps treat ovarian cysts. I was glad to figure out the problem and start treating it. When those things rupture, all the fluid stays inside and creates the risk of issues like pelvic inflammatory disease and other problems. So I was down for the Depo.

After a year or two had gone by, I went in for my OB/GYN check-up. The doctor asked me about my PCOS and checked in on things. "Are you wanting to stay on birth control?" she asked as she did the ultrasound.

"I want to stay on it," I said. "I'm not trying to have kids."

"Okay," she said, and didn't say more about it.

But after that, I did some more research into PCOS and learned that it's one of the leading causes of infertility. Not everyone with PCOS has a hard time getting pregnant. But in seventy-five percent of infertility cases where women aren't ovulating enough to conceive, PCOS is the cause. So the next time I talked to my OB, I asked, "Is this going to cause me any difficulty having kids down the line?"

"Well," she said, "Right now I wouldn't worry about it. Not everyone has that issue, and you're still young. Plus, you got pregnant before. Let's just cross that bridge when we get to it."

Fast forward a few years, and Taylor and I were starting to bounce around our hopes and dreams for the future. I was always upfront with him about my health issues. I wouldn't have wanted him to uproot his life and move to Chattanooga without knowing there was a chance that I might not ever be able to have another child of my own. I really wanted him to make a decision on his own behalf about whether or not he would be okay with that. If he wasn't, I wasn't going to hold it against him if he chose not to pursue our relationship any further.

"Nope," he said. Over and over, in his warm, laid-back way, he told me, "I would love to have a child on my own, and we can try. But that's not a deal breaker for me."

There had to be something wrong with Taylor. There had to be something I was missing, some catch. I kept waiting for the "uh-oh" moment, looking for the red flags, expecting to glimpse his dark side. But each day he just kept proving that he was exactly who he was. His warmth, wit, and calm just kept making my life better. It wasn't just that the way he treated me and Bentley was up to my standards. It was that he lived by his own standards. I didn't have to convince him to be caring, or helpful, or responsible. He was already like that when I found him, because that was the kind of person he was working to be.

In my other relationships, I was always struggling to pull the situation up to the level I believed I deserved. I had been raised to know my worth and to believe in a relationship defined by warmth,

affection, and mutual respect. So that was the only kind of relationship I was ever prepared to accept. And with the others, when
things got bad and I'd sit there alone at night pondering the state
of the union, one of the first things I'd ask myself was "Why are
you still here? Why aren't you leaving?" I was always checking in
with myself to make sure I remembered that I could leave if I
wanted to, and that I would find a healthier partnership with a man
who came closer to meeting the minimum standard of respect and
responsibility that I believed in.

I found that, and something even more profound. Or maybe
I just didn't know what it would feel like to be in the relationship I'd imagined for so long. Either way, it spun me around to
realize I'd started checking myself to make sure I was meeting
those standards. It was like I'd been trying to play ball with people
who couldn't throw the ball back and didn't care to figure it out.
For years I'd been on the field, throwing ball after ball, and never
getting it back. No matter how ready I was to play or how easy I
tried to make the game, the other players were more content to
kick the dirt around the field or go sit on the bench pretending
nobody ever told them the rules. So for seven years I got used to
just practicing my moves and waiting for a chance to play a decent
game.

Well, Taylor had arrived, and the game was on. Suddenly I had
someone in the batter's box who was excited to be there, ready to
play and eager to hit it out of the park. Finally I got to pitch and
catch and show off my best moves with someone who kept me on
my toes. Best of all, when I looked across the field, I found him
grinning at me like there was nowhere else he'd rather be.

Taylor's calm, kind reaction to my potential fertility issues left
me reassured that our future wouldn't be threatened by that possibility. Everything was still okay. For the time being, I was on birth

control. But since we were both clear on the fact that we'd love to bring another child into the picture someday if it were possible, I decided to get a better idea of what the status was. I was still young, but I wasn't getting any younger, and my basic understanding of fertility told me that the timeframe all women have to be aware of was probably different for people with PCOS. I wanted to be sure I understood the outlook.

So I got a reference for a fertility specialist and went in to ask for a full report. "How many eggs am I creating? How good are my chances? Give me the rundown." The specialist listened to my concerns, checked me out, and then sat me down to give it to me straight.

"You might as well go off birth control," she said, "because you're not creating any eggs."

It was a little shocking to hear. Obviously, I knew my PCOS came with issues, some of which were already very apparent. PCOS is related to hormonal imbalances. My body didn't make enough estrogen for ovulation, which was basically the root of my symptoms. But despite never having had regular periods, despite the fact that I hadn't been ovulating properly at the time, I'd gotten pregnant so quickly at sixteen that it seemed counterintuitive to question my fertility. The doctor I'd spoken to years before had seemed to agree, which was why I hadn't worried much about it since. When I told Taylor I might not be able to have more kids, I was more concerned with being honest and open with him about anything that could potentially affect our future. But it hadn't seemed pressing or probable enough for me to be anxious about it.

The doctor was very matter of fact. She told me that the outlook could change in the future, depending on what my body decided to do. But for now, my body just wasn't stocking the right ingredients for a pregnancy.

Taylor and I sat down and talked it over. We took as calm and realistic an approach as possible, and in the end, we came to two conclusions. First, there was no need for me to stay on birth control, because my body was being its own birth control. And second, if there was only a slim chance that we would ever be able to have kids together, we didn't want to stand in the way. We knew we wanted to get married. We knew we were in it for the long haul. And we knew as well as anyone that conceiving usually gets harder with age, not easier. And while I knew that birth control doesn't usually hurt fertility long term, I wasn't sure I liked the idea of messing with my already challenged hormones if I didn't have to. If we couldn't get pregnant five years down the line, we wouldn't want to look back and wonder if staying on birth control had anything to do with it.

So, we decided I'd stop taking birth control and see how the situation developed. In August, I went in for a normal checkup and found out that my blood work still didn't look promising. My white count was low, and my hormone levels were still completely out of whack. The signs seemed clear. My body was a No Pregnancy Zone. It was unsettling to hear such a bleak fertility forecast, but I tried to put it out of my mind. It wasn't like Taylor and I were desperate for a baby right at that moment. And if the outlook didn't improve and we got to feeling like we couldn't wait, we'd already decided we would be one hundred percent happy adopting a child. Whatever happened, it would be okay. So we just went with the flow.

One night we were hanging out, watching the Cowboys and drinking beer when I started to have these weird symptoms. My legs were getting tingly and itchy for no apparent reason, and my breasts felt tender. The tenderness in particular caught my attention. I mentioned it to Taylor and said, "Maybe I should take a pregnancy test, just in case."

"Yeah, maybe," he said. We were having another easygoing day. This barely made a ripple. When the game was over we got in the car with Bentley and swung by the store to pick up a pregnancy test, just as nonchalant as could be.

The line was faint, but the result was clear. I was pregnant.

We were completely shocked. We'd already given up on the possibility. I didn't even believe it until we went to the doctor to confirm it. She was just as shocked as we were, considering she'd been the one to tell us it wasn't likely to happen. Fortunately for her, we were absolutely pumped. Taylor was ready to fly around the moon, and I couldn't stop thinking, "This is amazing." I couldn't believe my body had come through and pulled off this miracle when I'd just about been ready to give up on it.

Of course, it also entered my mind right away that I'd spent the last seven years trying to get people away from unplanned pregnancy. So on that front I thought, "Shit. How am I going to handle this one?" But that wasn't nearly big enough of a problem to dampen the happiness, gratitude, and awe I felt.

It had been a long time since I was just a scared sixteen-year-old with no idea what to do and no partner to help me. Now I was a confident mom with an education, a career, and a partner who wanted to build a life with me — and understood what that meant. In fact, when I looked around at all the things that were different this time, it hit me that I'd made it to the other side of the mountain. Everything was different. It was warm and bright and full of hope, and the people I found there were strong, happy, and excited to be by my side.

I could barely believe I'd gotten to this place. I didn't have to be bulletproof anymore. Finally, I could just be Maci.

CHAPTER 24:

CALM SUMMER SKIES

At first, Bentley didn't believe I was pregnant. At all. Since I wasn't showing, he was very skeptical of the whole thing. But once he realized we weren't trying to trick him, he got excited and started sharing all his thoughts on being a big brother. Some days he wanted a brother, some days he wanted a sister, and some days he didn't care either way. We made a fun surprise out of telling him the baby's sex by having him cut into a cake full of pink frosting. Unfortunately, he happened to be in the mood for a brother that day. "Oh, man," he groaned when he saw the color. "A sister?" But once he got over the disappointment, he got on board and got excited.

I was excited for my pregnancy, especially for the ways it felt pleasantly different from the first time around. All the fear of what lay ahead was replaced by excitement. All the embarrassment was replaced by pride. All the concern from the people around me was replaced by celebration. I wasn't a "teen mom" this time. I was a grown woman and a confident parent. In a way, it felt like I was allowed to enjoy the experience in a way that hadn't been encouraged before.

And I was excited to have a family to share that enjoyment with me. It was nice to know that Bentley was old enough to do lots of things for himself and that he'd be a real part of my parenting experience, along with Taylor. I wasn't going back to those long, lonely nights when I'd sat in front of the TV feeling cut off from the rest of the world. It was difficult to believe that had ever been the case. When I looked back on it, I just had to shake my head at how far removed that reality was from what I'd achieved since then.

Taylor and I went on the hunt for a new house that would be big enough for me, him, Bentley, and Baby Number Two. It didn't take us long to find a place we liked, which was a relief, because we wanted to be settled by the time the baby came. We spent a weekend running around with realtors, and by the end we settled on a place that had everything we wanted and didn't need much work.

We made the move in April, with a couple of months of my third trimester to spare. The baby was due on June 12, so it was perfect timing. I was in the stage of pregnancy when my brain was going into nesting mode and all I wanted to do was clean and organize. This time around, I knew better than to stress myself out trying to get it all furnished and polished in two days, so I took it easy and just had fun preparing for my daughter.

Taylor and I wanted to be married, but we weren't about to rush it just because of the pregnancy. We wanted to focus on the pregnancy without the distraction of an engagement announcement and a wedding on the horizon. All that excitement could wait its turn. For now, we didn't want to cloud the experience and enjoyment of our first child together with any unnecessary extras. We figured we could tackle the wedding once we'd gotten the hang of parenting a newborn. In the meantime, the baby would have Taylor's last name.

We tossed a few names around before we settled on the right one. At first nothing was really sticking in our minds, but we kept going back to Jayde as a middle name. Eventually we realized, "If we like Jayde so much, why not make that the first name and look for a different middle name?"

We had also loved the name June, but since she was due in June, it seemed a little corny. But whenever I thought of it, I started thinking of June Carter Cash. So once I started trying to find something to go with Jayde, it popped back into my head. And there we had it: Jayde Carter.

Jayde Carter McKinney.

* * *

It was Bentley's first day of kindergarten. The whole school gathered in the cafeteria along with the teachers and parents, and then we all headed for the classrooms. I stayed with Bentley as the teacher explained a few basics, showed everyone where to hang up their things, and helped them find their seats. The parents were in there for about ten minutes as the kids settled in, and it was all fun and exciting until the teacher said, "Okay, time to tell your parents goodbye."

The look on Bentley's face was like a punch in the chest. The message in his eyes was loud and clear: Mom, what are you doing to me? You cannot leave me here with this strange woman and these weird kids. This is not okay.

Everyone warned me that this would be an emotional event, but I hadn't taken it too seriously. It was a big day, but I figured I'd survive in the usual fashion and be able to keep it together. I felt like I'd already been through it with preschool and daycare, and I was used to him being away for awhile every day. But they were right. This was bigger, and it was different, and I knew it the moment I saw that face. All of a sudden, I felt a huge wave of emotion rising up inside of me. It was unlike anything I'd ever felt. And right away, I knew I was going to lose it.

I managed to keep it together for as long as I was in the classroom, knowing it would only make him more upset to see me losing my cool. But as soon as I stepped out those doors, I fell apart. I made it outside, got in my car, and lost my damn mind.

I didn't even know why, exactly, I was crying. It just felt like I was drowning in emotion. Maybe it was the fact that he was in a real school where he'd be walking around right alongside the fifth graders, complete with a backpack full of books and an actual teacher. It wasn't like preschool or daycare. He wasn't just being babysat anymore, and you can't just skip kindergarten whenever you want. From now on, if I got a day off of work or we wanted to go on vacation, I couldn't just keep him to myself on a whim.

Bentley had just taken his first big step toward becoming an independent person. It was a whole new chapter for him. I couldn't have imagined how overwhelming it would be to witness that moment. The emotional reality was so intense it just swallowed me up. I sobbed all the way home. I hadn't cried so hard since the day I moved out of my parents house to live with Ryan. This was different. It wasn't fear or uncertainty that had me crying. This was a purer, more bittersweet mix of pride, joy, loss, worry, and excitement.

It was a new beginning for Bentley. And it was a new era for me, too. New beginnings were on the way for all of us. It felt like a tidal wave of change sweeping over me, leaving me with a new sense of past, present and future. I couldn't define each detail, but I felt the impact in my bones.

Once I got myself under control, I spent the day worrying about how he was liking kindergarten, if he was having fun, if he was bored, what he was doing. When I finally picked him up and asked how his day was, he said, "Kindergarten was even better than you told me it was gonna be."

Bentley took to school right away, except for the part where he has to wake up in the morning. His favorite subject turned out to be math, which blew my mind, because I've always been terrible with math and hated it with every bone in my body. But he's a smart kid. He takes his interests seriously and likes to excel at what he does. I don't remember being half as competitive as he is with baseball. But he's an easygoing kind of dude, too. He's not the type to run around talking to everyone in his class, but he opens up quickly when he senses someone shares his interests.

Sometimes I can see that he's got a bit of my loner streak. I'll ask him how his day is and he'll say, "It was good, but some of these kids get on my nerves." He gets frustrated when he wants to be alone and can't escape the company. But he fits in well, and he's popular with his teachers, which was a major concern of mine. I told him he could be a brat at home when he needs to as long as he keeps being an angel at school. It was an ego boost and a relief one day when I was dropping him off in the morning and a teacher stopped to tell me she thought the world of Bentley. She told me, "You're doing such a good job."

Thank God!

* * *

MTV was back on the scene for one last series following me and my original *Teen Mom* cast mates. Having the cameras around during my second pregnancy was a funny reminder of how much things had changed in the seven years since I'd first appeared on *16 & Pregnant*. That wasn't just true for me. When I looked around at the other girls and where their journeys had brought them, I got goosebumps. I knew each one of them had been down to the deepest, darkest depths of fear and uncertainty. I knew there had been a time for every one of them when they doubted they'd ever be okay. And I knew they'd pushed, dragged, crawled, and fought their way through those tunnels even when they couldn't see the lights at the other end.

It was awe-inspiring to look around at my fellow Teen Moms and see a group of real life adults with beautiful, healthy kids and big hopes for the future. Between the four of us, we'd weathered millions of doubts and judgments. Some of us definitely got rained on harder than others. But there we were, seven years later, blowing even our own expectations out of the water. When I looked around at what we'd survived and the strong, capable people we'd become, my heart just swelled with pride and respect. The Teen Moms had made it.

What I learned through my experiences with MTV, and what I taught myself along the way, helped me get a job as a social media marketing specialist. I absolutely loved it. It was something I could see myself doing just about anywhere. The world of social media is changing all the time, and it's a challenge to keep up with what's relevant. You're constantly studying and analyzing how people spend time online and where brands stand the best chance of making money. There's a ton of tracking and analytics that you have to do to be able to prove to your boss that the brands are getting something out of social media. I never pictured myself as an eight to five, sit at your desk all day type of person, and if anyone had asked me two years before if I saw myself in a job like that, I'd tell them they were insane. But it turned out to be really engaging work for me, different and dynamic every day.

With just a few months left before Jayde Carter's arrival, I finally graduated from Chattanooga State Community College with my media technology degree, along with a minor in creative writing. Five years of going back and forth, juggling those classes and reminding myself that "Mom did it" had finally paid off, and not a moment too soon.

When I found out I was pregnant at sixteen, the list of challenges I needed to overcome was almost too overwhelming to think about. Any time I had tried to take a mental survey of the things I needed to change and accomplish if I wanted a happy, fulfilling life for myself and my child, my brain just fizzled out and shut down. The scale of everything I had to do was just incomprehensible. So instead of trying to comprehend it, I just looked straight ahead and kept putting one foot in front of the other. It wasn't until I checked off the last item on my Teen Mom To Do List that I was able to turn around and look back over what I had accomplished.

Nothing good comes easy. There may be days when fortune seems to fall in your lap, and you look around and can't figure out how you got so lucky. There may be times when you try your best and can't come up with anything but frustration and failure. But at the end of the day, what you get out of your life depends on what you put into it. The more you take care of the good things in your life, the longer they stick around and the better they become. The more you persevere in the face of doubt and discouragement, the stronger you become. The harder you work for the things you want, the more they mean to you when you find them.

Whenever I look back over the peaks, valleys, and battlefields I crossed to get where I wanted to be, I feel calm, confident, and grateful for the gifts I found along the way. I'll never know where exactly my life would have gone if I'd taken any other path. But I do know that the journey pushed me to become the Maci I want to be. The struggles fade into the past. But the strength and sense of self I earned by overcoming them will help me for the rest of my life.

The sun is shining on the road ahead. That could change in the blink of an eye. If it does, I'll handle it. But as long as the skies are calm, I'll be making the most of it with my family, my friends, and my children.

I proved to myself that I can be bulletproof. Now, it's time to be happy.

CHAPTER 25:

AN UPDATE FROM MACI

When I look back on the life I wrote about in this book, it is crazy to see how different things are. My story has taken some twists and turns, but it's all been for the better.

In early 2016, Taylor, Bentley, Jayde, and I made a trip to Los Angeles to do some filming and media events for *Teen Mom OG*. One of the days we were there, Taylor and I went to Venice Beach where we were going to film the reunion show for the latest season—or so I thought. Before we filmed, he and I drove out to the beach to do a photo shoot for MTV.com. The photographer had us do a bunch of cool off-the-wall poses. We weren't doing any typical couple pictures, but then he told us to face each other and get close, which I thought was kind of odd. Taylor looked at me and said, "Hey, I have to ask you a question." I thought, *What on earth could he want right now in the middle of this shoot?*

"Now is not the time," I said, thinking he was going to ask me something about when we had to be back at the studio or what we should do that night. Instead, he got down one knee and said, "Will you marry me?" I was completely surprised. I had no idea he had planned to propose, which is really saying something because I usually know when something is up. After I got over the shock, I said "Of course!" and then . . . "Finally!" My heart was racing and

I was over the moon. After waiting so long for Taylor to propose, it turned out to be the perfect moment.

From there, we left the beach to go to an end-of-season wrap party—again, so I thought. It turned out to be a surprise engagement party for Taylor and me. I hadn't seen Bentley yet to tell him the news and I was so excited to see his reaction. He was waiting for us at the party and when we told him, he was so happy that he actually started crying. It was so sweet.

* * *

Not long after we celebrated our engagement, we were back in Tennessee getting back to life as usual. I had been on birth control ever since we had Jayde and had an appointment to go back to the doctor to renew my prescription. Everything was looking normal until the doctor left the room for a while. When she came back in she looked at me and said, "I can't give you any more birth control because you are pregnant." I laughed and thought she was just messing with me. But she kept a serious look on her face and said she wasn't kidding. I blurted out, "You've got to have someone else's test results then. There is no way I'm pregnant." She showed me the results that proved it. I was in total disbelief. It felt like everything left my body and I had been completely drained. The doctor said their ultrasound technician was free and asked if I wanted to go look at the baby and see how far along I was. It felt like I floated into the next room and before I knew it, I was lying down and looking at my third baby. Sure enough, I was pregnant.

Once I could think again, I started worrying about all the practicalities. I hadn't had any symptoms at all and I've never had a regular cycle because of my struggles with polycystic ovarian syndrome. So I was definitely not treating my body like I was pregnant. I was so scared that something might be wrong with the baby, but the technician told me everything looked normal and healthy. Thank God.

Then she turned to me and said, "So, do you want to know if it's a boy or a girl?"

Excuse me? I thought. Was I seriously far along enough to tell the sex of the baby?

"You're measuring at about twenty weeks," the technician said. She must have picked up on how crazy I felt, because she asked if I was okay.

"No, I'm actually not okay," I said. "I just found out I'm pregnant *today!*"

It was all so unexpected. Luckily, Taylor and Bentley had come to my appointment because we had to do something afterwards, and they were able to see the baby, too. They were both so excited, especially after we found out the baby was a boy.

After talking to my doctor during another appointment, I mentioned how strange it was that I hadn't had any symptoms, especially because I always know what's going on with my body. I had known within six weeks that I was pregnant with Bentley and Jayde. Why did this time feel so different?

It turns out, she explained, that I had gotten pregnant so soon after I had Jayde that my body hadn't had time to adjust to being not pregnant. Those same hormones that I'd developed while carrying Jayde had just stayed and nothing went back to normal. So I had actually never even had the chance to feel the symptoms of pregnancy. Go figure.

It took me a while to recover from feeling like a bus had hit me. Taylor and I had always talked about having a third child, but we were considering adoption. My family's excitement helped a lot, and soon I was just as excited. Bentley had also always wanted a little brother to play baseball with, so we were happy he was getting one to coach.

This time around, my pregnancy was much harder than the two I'd been through before, only because I had a crazy almost-one-year-old to keep an eye on. When I was pregnant with Jayde, Bentley was old enough to take care of himself—he knew how to brush his teeth, get dressed, take a shower, pour himself a bowl of cereal in the morning. Even after Jayde was born, his maturity made taking care of a newborn much easier. But Jayde, at eleven months old, was running everywhere and getting in to everything, and I had to chase her around like an insane person. After going through that experience, I will always say that I would much rather have a newborn and a one-year-old than be extremely pregnant with a one-year-old. It was exhausting.

But of course, it was all worth it. Our son Maverick Reed came into the world on May 31st, just two days after Jayde's first birthday. Our family felt instantly complete.

***

Adjusting to being a parent of three kids was harder than I thought, but Taylor and I make a great team. He is a wonderful father, and is always hands-on and involved in every aspect of their lives. There is no way I would be able to do this without him—he makes everything easier and we're constantly asking how we can help each other. We both try to look at everything in a positive way: hey, at least we're constantly entertained, are never bored, and have fun. Life is nothing short of chaotic, but we will always find a way to make it work.

We even miraculously found time to go in on a clothing company called Things That Matter with a couple of our friends who are also investors. Owning a clothing line was always something Taylor wanted to do and we're both really happy with the outcome. Thankfully, we were able to make TTM into something big pretty quickly, but it's definitely been a learning experience. Taylor has even taken on the clothing line full time, which has been a dream come true for him. I will always consider myself lucky that I can call my life partner my business partner, and that we're able to balance everything while keeping our priorities straight, too.

MTV and *Teen Mom* is obviously still a huge part of my life. There was a stretch of time where I felt very protective over Bentley and didn't want his life to be in the spotlight. It was hard for me when it felt like we couldn't go anywhere without my young son being recognized from a TV show. I wanted to give him a normal childhood. But now, I realize that we would never have an ordinary life even if we weren't on the show. We've been doing this for eight years now and we'll never be "normal" again, so I've completely embraced it. This is our life and my family is happy and healthy, and that's what matters.

* * *

When I wrote this book, the word "bulletproof" meant a lot to me as an individual. I used it as a tool to get myself through some really difficult times, but I've come a long way since then. I have a wonderful man in my life, three beautiful children, and an amazing career. But being bulletproof doesn't mean that I won't ever get hurt or make mistakes or get scared. It simply means that I need to remember my self-worth and remember that I matter.

That is the most important lesson I want to instill in Bentley, Jayde, and Maverick. I want to teach them how to find their self-esteem on their own and how to build it up and keep it. I never want them to go a day without knowing that they matter. Maybe one day they'll have to go through times that are just as hard as mine were, if not harder. Feeling alone sometimes is normal, but I will do my damnedest to make sure they know they're not alone and they never will be. I learned at just sixteen years old that when you feel lost in the midst of this crazy world, that's when you really find yourself. I hope they take chances, make themselves a priority, and know when to follow their gut and when to follow their heart. And I hope each of my children knows how to be independent and not rely on someone else for their happiness.

I know that, at some point, things will become difficult again. When that time comes, I won't be alone. I will have my family, and *together* we will be bulletproof.